Jonathan's
BLUEGRASS TABLE
REDEFINING KENTUCKY CUISINE

For Chris,
"Enjoy the Bluegrass!"

Jon Jaff 2010

Jonathan's
BLUEGRASS TABLE
REDEFINING KENTUCKY CUISINE

JONATHAN LUNDY
PHOTOGRAPHY BY LEE THOMAS

BUTLER BOOKS
LOUISVILLE, KENTUCKY

ISBN 978-1-935497-10-3
Printed in Canada

For additional information, contact:
Jonathan Lundy
www.jagp.info
www.jonathanlundy.com

Photography © 2009 by Lee Thomas
www.leethomasphotography.com

Book design by Scott Stortz

Published by:

Butler Books
P.O. Box 7311
Louisville, KY 40207
(502) 897–9393
Fax (502) 897–9797

www.butlerbooks.com

Acknowledgments

My Parents
Louis J. Roussel III
Emeril Lagasse
Roy Meyers
The Staff of Jonathan at Gratz Park
Charlie Stone
Paul Sanders
Leon and Sandy Hollon
Greg and Becky Goodman
Lee and Janet Thomas

Most of all, my best friend, business partner and wife
Cara

Table of Contents

Introduction

CHAPTER ONE
Gracious Greens

CHAPTER TWO
More Than Burgoo

CHAPTER THREE
Southern-Inspired Starters

CHAPTER FOUR
It's Suppertime!

CHAPTER FIVE
Bluegrass Brunches

CHAPTER SIX
Our Daily Bread

CHAPTER SEVEN
Jonathan's Signature Sides

CHAPTER EIGHT
Dramatic Endings

CHAPTER NINE
Un-Commonwealth Cocktails

Index

Introduction

My earliest memories of cooking go back to my grandfather, who was not generally known for his cooking skills. He would, however, cook for me and he always made biscuits and gravy. I would watch him in awe as he would make the dough from memory, roll it and cut it out. Next, he browned the sausage in a large skillet, then he poured the simple pan gravy over steaming, fork-split biscuits.

From then on, I wanted to cook. I wanted to create in others the same excitement and joy I felt in those moments. The time spent with my grandfather, John Henry Lundy, enjoying his biscuits and gravy, taught me the essence and importance of family and Southern hospitality.

I was raised in Midway, Kentucky, a small town located in central Kentucky's Bluegrass Region. My family has had strong roots within the Bluegrass for many generations – on my father's side, a legacy of agricultural farming; and on my mother's side, a thoroughbred horse dynasty, as well as the invention of Calumet baking powder.

As a young man, I was fortunate enough to travel extensively with my family. That opportunity allowed me to discover new foods and their preparation. It fueled and diversified my interest in cooking, as did my first kitchen job as an apprentice to the iconic Chef Emeril Lagasse. I followed in his footsteps by enrolling in the culinary program at Johnson and Wales University.

Once back in Kentucky, I worked for the next five years as the chef in a local independent restaurant. The restaurant was fast-paced and had an exciting "fusion" menu. But in the end, none of these wonderful experiences led me away from my first desire: to further my knowledge of the traditional foods that I grew up eating as a child – the foods of Kentucky.

In 1998, my wife Cara and I opened Jonathan at Gratz Park. From the very beginning, our concept for the restaurant was to blend the traditional flavors of the Bluegrass with modern world cuisine. The restaurant is located in Lexington, Kentucky's downtown Gratz Park district, situated within the historic Gratz Park Inn, a small boutique inn known for its blend of classical appeal with modern amenities, as well as its distinctly Southern grace and charm. From this location we continue to blend influences for our varied clientele. We have a strong local following and a constant flow of national and international visitors.

The Bluegrass Region of Kentucky occupies a distinctive place in the American imagination – a place of undulating hills, horses and bourbon distilleries. From our front porch swings, we enjoy sunsets over fields of sweet corn, sorghum and soybeans. Food and animal feed crops have replaced much of the traditional tobacco base, and farmers markets have found permanent homes in the cities. There is nothing like a Kentucky tomato or local wildflower honey. Pork has reached near-cult level – country hams, jowl bacon – there is simply none better. The same limestone base that nurtures the thoroughbred horses here also imparts its richness to grass-fed lamb, cattle and goats, whose milk has inspired local cheese artisans. A sixth-generation mill still grinds local corn and wheat just up the creek from where I played as a child. *Jonathan's Bluegrass Table* is part of this story.

My redefined Bluegrass cuisine was developed to be experimental and fun. I encourage readers to enjoy the cooking process, as well as the time spent with family and friends while dining. Remember, cooking should be fun. These recipes should not be treated as a textbook, but rather as an inspiration in the development of your own creative cooking skills. Feel free to make substitutions and add personal touches. Don't be afraid to make mistakes. Some of my best recipes were perfected by what I thought was an error. Enjoy!

Gracious Greens

Bright, fresh and crisp greens are graciously introduced to sweet, salty or crunchy flavors in these surprising salads. Play with the ideas yourself. All were inspired by my childhood avoidance of anything green.

Crunchy, cornmeal-Fried Green Tomatoes – a Southern original – are paired with the buttery, tender Bluegrass original, Limestone Bibb lettuce tossed with Buttermilk Dressing. I stack the tomatoes with layers of the lettuce and then cut the stack in half to display the delicious contrast of the light green insides and the surrounding golden crust.

In my Cayenne Pecan Brittle Salad, bitter flavored greens are balanced by the sweetness of fresh Peach Preserve Vinaigrette. The spicy crunch of my Cayenne Pecan Brittle adds just a counterpoint of kick.

For my version of a classic Caesar Salad, I grill half-heads of Romaine lettuce rubbed with freshly made Caesar Salad Dressing. The grilled lettuce is then chopped, so that the slightly-wilted smoky charred texture of the outer leaves blends with the sweet crunch of the inner leaves. An earthy, nutty Parmigiano-Reggiano and my Crispy Black-Eyed Peas round out these flavors. This is a great salad to add to … grilled chicken, sliced porterhouse steak, butter-roasted shrimp, cracker-fried oysters… endless possibilities, all good.

In the warm spring and summer months, my Chicken Salad-Stuffed Tomato with chilled asparagus and Pickled Pepper Vinaigrette is a perfect main course for a Bluegrass ladies luncheon. I am often experimental with food, but when it comes to Chicken Salad, I remain a traditionalist with just the simplest of ingredients. The Pickled Pepper Vinaigrette fully embraces the Kentucky affection for banana peppers.

I like to hot-smoke salmon using Maker's Mark barrel plugs. That smoky bourbon note combined with the maple syrup in my Maple-Mustard Vinaigrette just evokes the October Keeneland race meet and falling leaves. Don't skimp on the Cornbread Croutons.

The Shrimp Corn Dog Wedge Salad – cornmeal-and-beer-battered fried shrimp with chilled iceberg lettuce and my Deviled Thousand Island Dressing – is County Fair, upgraded. Whimsy is good.

Shrimp Corn Dogs also make a great appetizer, with a little hot mustard.

Kentucky Hot Slaw, original to northern Kentucky, is a warm salad perfect for chilly evenings. My adaptation slow-simmers cabbage, bell peppers, onions and bacon in a dressing of cider vinegar, brown sugar and pork jowl drippings. Pork Jowl Cracklings garnish the slaw.

Play and have fun with your greens. If you keep the components fresh and flavor-packed, even the youngest members of your family can find salads exciting.

GRACIOUS GREENS

Fried Green Tomato Salad

Fried Green Tomatoes
Buttermilk Dressing

Cayenne Pecan Brittle Salad

Cayenne Pecan Brittle
Peach Preserves
Peach Preserve Vinaigrette

Grilled Caesar Salad

Caeser Salad Dressing
Crispy Black-Eyed Peas

Hot Smoked Salmon Chop Salad

Maple-Mustard Hot Smoked Salmon
Maple-Mustard Glaze
Maple-Mustard Dressing
Cornbread Croutons

Chicken Salad-Stuffed Tomato with Pickled Pepper-Marinated Asparagus

Pickled Pepper Vinaigrette
Chicken Salad

Shrimp Corn Dog Wedge Salad

Shrimp Corn Dogs
Kentucky Ale Batter
Deviled Thousand Island Dressing

Kentucky Hot Slaw

Hot Slaw Dressing
Pork Jowl Cracklings

Fried Green Tomato Salad

INGREDIENTS

2 heads Limestone
Bibb lettuce

12 slices Fried Green
Tomatoes (page 17)

6 ounces Buttermilk
Dressing (page 18)

½ cup sliced bacon,
cooked crisp

2 tablespoons
small-diced, roasted
red bell peppers

METHOD

1) Wash Bibb lettuce in cool water and shake off excess water.

2) Remove 8 outer leaves of Bibb and set aside. Slice the remaining lettuce into ¼-inch ribbons and place in salad mixing bowl.

3) Prepare Fried Green Tomatoes with recipe provided.

4) Toss the cut Bibb lettuce with about 4 ounces of the Buttermilk Dressing.

5) Place 4 Fried Green Tomatoes on a cutting board and place approximately ⅛ of the dressing-tossed lettuce on each of the 4 Fried Green Tomatoes. Top each with another Fried Green Tomato. Repeat process. When finished, you will have 4 stacks of 3 Fried Green Tomatoes, each with 2 layers of Buttermilk Dressing-tossed Bibb lettuce ribbons.

6) Place 2 of the outer whole Bibb lettuce leaves in the center of 4 plates.

7) Slice each green tomato stack in half and carefully place the 2 halves on each plate, with the cut side facing up.

8) Garnish the salads with the remaining Buttermilk Dressing and a pinch of the diced roasted red bell peppers.

9) Top off the center of each salad with about a tablespoon of crispy bacon.

SERVES 4

Fried Green Tomatoes

INGREDIENTS

4-6 green tomatoes

4 tablespoons kosher salt

2 cups flour

5 eggs

1½ cups milk

4 cups yellow cornmeal

1 teaspoon garlic powder

1 teaspoon onion powder

2 teaspoons salt

1 teaspoon fresh
ground black pepper

½ teaspoon dried sage

1 teaspoon dried thyme

¼ teaspoon
cayenne powder

1 cup vegetable oil

Pairing notes: *Fried Green Tomato Salad: Limestone Bibb lettuce, Applewood Smoked Bacon and Buttermilk Dressing*

METHOD

1) Slice the green tomatoes into ¼-inch slices. Lay sliced tomatoes on a sheet tray or baking sheet. Sprinkle the 4 tablespoons kosher salt evenly over the tomatoes. Let the tomatoes sit at room temperature for 1 hour. Salt will draw out excess moisture from the tomatoes. Set tomatoes aside.

2) Place flour in a medium-size bowl. Set aside.

3) Mix eggs and milk together thoroughly. Set aside.

4) In a large mixing bowl, mix the remainder of the ingredients together. Set aside.

5) In a large skillet, preheat vegetable oil to 350 degrees Fahrenheit.

6) Dust green tomatoes in the flour. One at a time, dip the tomatoes in the egg and milk mixture, then transfer into the cornmeal mixture. Repeat process until all tomatoes are breaded in the cornmeal.

7) Place a few green tomatoes in the skillet at a time and sauté for about 2-3 minutes on each side. Remove from pan and place on a tray lined with paper towels. Repeat until all tomatoes are cooked.

SERVES 6

Buttermilk Dressing

INGREDIENTS

1 tablespoon diced
yellow onions

½ tablespoon
Dijon mustard

⅓ cup cider vinegar

¾ cup buttermilk

¼ tablespoon
buttermilk powder

¼ cup sour cream

½ cup mayonnaise

pinch of
cayenne powder

⅛ teaspoon ground
white pepper

¼ tablespoon salt

⅔ cup vegetable oil

METHOD

1) Place diced onions, Dijon mustard and cider vinegar in a food processor and purée until a smooth consistency is achieved.

2) Add all other ingredients except the vegetable oil and purée until smooth.

3) While food processor is running, slowly drizzle in oil to form an emulsion.

4) Store in refrigerator until served.

5) Can be made up to 2 days ahead of time.

YIELDS ABOUT 2 ½ CUPS

Pairing notes: *Fried Green Tomatoes, Limestone Bibb lettuce and Applewood Smoked Bacon.*

Cooking notes:
Buttermilk powder is used for bread baking and is available in the baking section in most grocery stores.

Cayenne Pecan Brittle Salad

INGREDIENTS

8 cups mixed salad greens

6 ounces Peach Preserve
Vinaigrette (page 23)

12 ounces goat cheese

1 ½ cups crumbled
Cayenne Pecan Brittle
(page 22)

2 tablespoons diced,
roasted red bell pepper

METHOD

1) Wash salad greens in cool water. Use salad spinner to remove
   excess water.
2) Place greens into a large salad bowl and toss with about
   6 ounces Peach Preserve Vinaigrette.
3) Divide the greens among the serving plates.
4) Top off each salad with crumbled goat cheese, brittle
   and roasted red bell pepper for garnish.
5) Drizzle the remaining dressing on plate to garnish.

SERVES 4-6

Cayenne Pecan Brittle

INGREDIENTS

2 teaspoons salt

2 teaspoons baking soda

¼ teaspoon
cayenne powder

2 cups sugar

1 cup corn syrup

½ cup water

½ pound butter

3 cups chopped pecans

METHOD

1) Mix together the salt, baking soda and cayenne pepper.

2) In a 4-quart pot, add sugar, corn syrup, water and stir well. Place pot on medium heat and bring to a boil.

3) Stir in butter.

4) Using a candy thermometer, continue to boil the mixture until the liquid reaches 305 degrees Fahrenheit. This should take 10-15 minutes.

5) Remove from heat and quickly stir in the salt mixture.

6) Stir in pecans.

7) Dump out onto a sheet tray.

8) Allow the mixture to cool and harden. Break into bite-size pieces.

9) Store in an airtight container for up to 1 week.

YIELDS 2½ POUNDS

Pairing notes: *Bitter greens with goat cheese and Cayenne Pecan Brittle*

Cooking notes:
Be careful not to over-cook the sugar. If you do, it will result in an unusable burnt flavor.

Peach Preserves

Homemade fresh fruit preserves can be enjoyed with breakfast, or used as an ingredient in other recipes. This base recipe is an ingredient in the Peach Preserve Vinaigrette and also Peach Sweet-and-Sour Sauce (page 82).

INGREDIENTS

4 cups sliced, pitted and peeled peaches (about 3 pounds whole peaches)

2 tablespoons freshly-squeezed lemon juice

1 package (1.75 oz) Sure-Jell fruit pectin

5 cups sugar

METHOD

1) Place the lemon juice and peaches into a 4-quart saucepan over high heat.

2) When the mixture starts to boil, add the fruit pectin and stir.

3) When mixture begins to boil again, add the sugar and stir until fully incorporated.

4) Allow mixture to return to a boil and continue boiling for one full minute.

5) Remove from heat and let cool to room temperature.

6) Store in an airtight container in the refrigerator.

7) This recipe can be made up to 2 weeks ahead of time.

YIELDS 7 CUPS

Peach Preserve Vinaigrette

This simple vinaigrette made with fresh Peach Preserves is extremely easy and delicious and pairs with an array of salad greens.

INGREDIENTS

½ cup Peach Preserves (recipe above)

½ cup cider vinegar

1 ½ cups vegetable oil

METHOD

1) Place the preserves and vinegar into a food processor and purée until smooth.

2) While machine is running, very slowly add the oil.

3) Store in the refrigerator.

YIELDS 2½ CUPS

Pairing notes: Bitter greens with Peach Preserve Vinaigrette, goat cheese and Cayenne Pecan Brittle.

Cooking notes: Store-bought peach preserves can be substituted. Experiment with a variety of types of jams, jellies and preserves.

Grilled Caesar Salad

This one-of-a-kind twist on a traditional Caesar salad makes a great appetizer or a light entrée salad. Grilling the Romaine lettuce quickly adds another dimension. The outer layers become slightly charred while the insides stay cool and crisp. The addition of Crispy Black-Eyed Peas provides textural excitement. Store-bought dressing can be substituted for homemade Caesar salad dressing, if necessary.

INGREDIENTS

3 whole heads of Romaine lettuce

3 cups Jonathan's Caesar Salad Dressing (page 26)

1 cup shredded Parmesan cheese

½ cup diced roasted red peppers

2 cups Crispy Black-Eyed Peas (page 27)

Pairing notes: Grilled Caesar Salad with Parmesan cheese and Crispy Black-Eyed Peas. The salad can be topped off with grilled chicken, shrimp or beef, if desired.

Cooking notes: Have a little water nearby that can be used to help prevent flame-ups on the grill, which will have an undesirable effect on the flavor of the salad. The dressing is what would burn, so be sure to use lightly.

METHOD

1) Remove outer layers of the lettuce. Place on cutting board and cut the whole head in half from top to bottom.

2) Submerge into ice water and soak for a few minutes.

3) Remove from water and shake off excess liquid.

4) Stand half-heads core side down and refrigerate. This can be done up to one day in advance and will allow almost all of the water to drain from the lettuce.

5) Preheat grill and allow fire to burn down. Hold your hand 5 inches over the grill. If you cannot comfortably keep your hand above the fire for more than 5 seconds, then the grill is too hot. Allow 5-10 minutes for fire to reduce in heat.

6) Place the half-heads of Romaine on a tray and rub the dressing lightly on the outer layers of the lettuce. Be sure to get both the tops and bottoms.

7) Place the lettuce inner-side down on grill. Cook for about 2 minutes. Do not flip over and cook outer side of the Romaine.

8) Remove from grill and place on a cutting board and cut each half into quarters. Remove the core from the Romaine.

9) Place the 2 quarters on the plate, slightly overlapping for each serving.

10) Drizzle more dressing over Romaine, and garnish with the peppers, Parmesan cheese and Crispy Black-Eyed Peas.

S E R V E S   6

Caesar Salad Dressing

This is an easy homemade Caesar salad dressing used for Grilled Caesar Salad. The dressing is equally delicious with traditional Caesar salad as well.

INGREDIENTS

10 coddled eggs
(You will only need 8 yolks for dressing, but coddle 2 extra)

10 cloves raw garlic, minced

2 teaspoons salt

8 teaspoons freshly-squeezed lemon juice

4 teaspoons Worcestershire sauce

½ teaspoon Tabasco

10 anchovy fillets

4 teaspoons red wine vinegar

2 teaspoons Dijon mustard

8 teaspoons finely-grated Parmesan cheese

1 teaspoon freshly-ground black pepper

2 cups extra virgin olive oil

METHOD

1) In a medium-sized pot, bring 2 quarts water to a boil. Carefully place 10 whole eggs into the water. Boil the eggs for 2 minutes. Remove eggs from water. Place eggs on a tray and put into the refrigerator.

2) Once the eggs are fully cooled, crack them open and remove the yolks. Discard the shells and the whites. Place the yolk into the refrigerator for up to 1 hour before making the dressing.

3) Place 8 coddled egg yolks and other ingredients except the olive oil in a food processor and purée. Stop the processor, scrape down the sides and purée again. Repeat this process until mixture is smooth.

4) Turn food processor on again and slowly drizzle the olive oil into the machine to form an emulsion.

5) Dressing can be made ahead and stored in a refrigerator for up to 1 hour before being served.

6) If dressing is too thick, whisk in a few drops of warm water to thin out the consistency.

YIELDS 3 CUPS

Pairing notes: *Grilled Caesar Salad with Parmesan cheese and Crispy Black-Eyed Peas*

Cooking notes: *The eggs and part of the whites will be cooked, but the yolk should still be runny. The coddling process is done to reduce the risk of food-borne illness associated with consuming raw egg yolks. The recipe calls for 8 coddled egg yolks, but I suggest you coddle 10. It is a good idea to have extra in case you drop or damage some.*

Crispy Black-Eyed Peas

Black-eyed peas are as Southern as it gets. I have developed a new method to prepare this Southern classic into a one-of-a-kind accompaniment.

INGREDIENTS

3 cups dried
black-eyed peas

6 cups water

1 tablespoon iodized salt

½ teaspoon garlic powder

½ teaspoon onion powder

½ teaspoon finely-ground
black pepper

METHOD

1) In a gallon container, place the black-eyed peas and water and soak for at least 24 hours.

2) Dump the soaked peas and water into a colander in a sink. Allow peas to thoroughly drain. Using paper towels, pat the peas down to remove all water. The peas must be totally dry before the next step.

3) Place 6 cups of vegetable oil into a small table-top deep fat fryer or a large pot and preheat it to 300 degrees Fahrenheit.

4) Mix dried spices and salt together in a small bowl.

5) In small batches, add the peas to the oil and fry for about 10-12 minutes or until they turn a light tan color. Remove peas from oil with a slotted spoon or small, fine mesh hand-held strainer. Place the cooked peas onto a paper towel-lined sheet tray.

6) While the peas are still warm, season with dried spices and salt.

7) Allow to cool, then store at room temperature in an airtight container for up to 2 weeks.

YIELDS ABOUT 8 CUPS

Hot Smoked Salmon Chop Salad

INGREDIENTS

8 cups chopped
Romaine lettuce

½ cup shredded
white cheddar cheese

½ cup diced tomatoes

4 diced hard-boiled eggs

½ cup Cornbread Croutons
(page 31)

8 ounces Maple-Mustard
Dressing (page 31)

1 pound Maple-Mustard
Hot Smoked Salmon
(page 30)

METHOD

1) Wash chopped Romaine in cool water. Use salad spinner to remove excess water.

2) In a large salad bowl, mix all ingredients.

3) Divide salad onto salad plates.

4) Top salads with smoked salmon.

SERVES 4-6

Maple-Mustard Hot Smoked Salmon

INGREDIENTS

1 cup Maple-Mustard Glaze (recipe below)

1 ½ pounds fresh salmon, boned and skinned, cut into 6 4-ounce fillets.

METHOD

1) Make Maple-Mustard Glaze.

2) Lay out fresh salmon on a sheet tray and spread the glaze over the salmon.

3) Smoke the salmon in a smoker, following manufacturer's directions. If using a low temperature smoker (below 90 degrees Fahrenheit), smoke the salmon for about 15 minutes and finish cooking salmon in a 350-degree Fahrenheit oven. Salmon should be slightly undercooked to be at its best. If using a higher temperature smoker (120 degrees Fahrenheit), then allow the salmon to smoke and cook for about 15-20 minutes.

SERVES 6

Maple-Mustard Glaze

INGREDIENTS

3 tablespoons whole grain mustard

5 tablespoons real maple syrup

½ cup Dijon mustard

½ teaspoon salt

¼ teaspoon freshly-ground pepper

METHOD

1) Mix the whole grain mustard, Dijon, maple syrup, salt and pepper together in a small bowl.

2) Store in a refrigerator until needed. Can be made up to 1 week ahead of time.

YIELDS 1 CUP

Maple-Mustard Dressing

INGREDIENTS

1 tablespoon
small-diced yellow onion

½ tablespoon
Dijon mustard

¼ cup real maple syrup

¼ cup cider vinegar

1 teaspoon
whole grain mustard

¼ cup mayonnaise

½ tablespoon brown sugar

½ teaspoon salt

¼ teaspoon freshly-
ground black pepper

¾ cup vegetable oil

METHOD

1) Place all ingredients except oil in food processor, and purée until smooth.
2) Slowly add oil, while machine is running, to form an emulsion.
3) Store in a refrigerator for up to 1 week.

YIELDS 4 CUPS

Cornbread Croutons

INGREDIENTS

4 cups leftover or day-old
Southern Cornbread
(page 163)

2 tablespoons
melted butter

METHOD

1) Preheat oven to 300 degrees Fahrenheit.
2) Dice cornbread into ½-inch cubes.
3) Place in a mixing bowl and toss with melted butter.
4) Pour out onto a sheet pan and bake for about 20-25 minutes or until they start to get crispy.
5) Remove from oven and allow to cool.

YIELDS 4 CUPS

Chicken Salad-Stuffed Tomato with Pickled Pepper-Marinated Asparagus

INGREDIENTS

2 ¼ pounds (4 ½ cups) Chicken Salad (page 35)

3 medium-sized tomatoes, crowned

3 cups mixed baby greens

24 blanched fresh asparagus spears

24 French bread toast points

1½ cups Pickled Pepper Vinaigrette (page 34)

METHOD

1) Divide mixed greens among 6 serving plates, placing greens in center of plate. Top greens with half-tomato crown.

2) Place half-tomato crown in center of mixed greens. Top each tomato with equal portions of chicken salad.

3) Pierce each chicken salad portion with four toast points. Place four chilled asparagus spears in between each toast point, with asparagus tips pointing up.

4) Ladle Pickled Pepper Vinaigrette on asparagus and around edge of plate.

SERVES 6

Pickled Pepper Vinaigrette

INGREDIENTS

½ cup drained and puréed pickled banana peppers

⅛ cup puréed yellow onions, well-drained

½ cup apple cider vinegar

½ tablespoon sugar

¼ teaspoon salt

¼ tablespoon ground white pepper

1½ cups olive oil

METHOD

1) Place all ingredients except olive oil in a blender and purée until smooth.

2) While machine is running, slowly add the olive oil to form an emulsion.

3) Store in a refrigerator for up to 1 week.

YIELDS ABOUT 2½ CUPS

Chicken Salad

INGREDIENTS

4-6 bone-in, skin-on split
chicken breasts

4 cups water

1 cup finely-diced
yellow onion

1 cup finely-diced celery

1 tablespoon
Dijon mustard

¾ -1 cup mayonnaise

1 tablespoon
chicken cooking liquid

½ teaspoon salt

¼ teaspoon
ground white pepper

½ teaspoon
chopped fresh thyme

METHOD

1) Place raw chicken breasts and the water in a small pot and bring to a boil. Boil for 1 full minute. Turn heat off and cover with a lid and allow to cool to room temperature, about 20-25 minutes.

2) Remove chicken from cooking liquid. Remove skin and discard. Pick meat from the bones, using your hands, and pull the meat into small, bite-size pieces. You should end up with about 4 cups.

3) Mix all ingredients together.

4) Store in a refrigerator for up to 3 days.

SERVES 6

Shrimp Corn Dog Wedge Salad

INGREDIENTS

2 heads iceberg lettuce

4 ripe tomatoes

Salt and pepper,
as needed

8 hard-boiled eggs

1 red onion

16 Shrimp Corn Dogs
(pages 38-39)

Deviled Thousand Island
Dressing, (page 41)

METHOD

1) Prepare Deviled Thousand Island Dressing and Kentucky Ale Batter ahead of time. Refrigerate until ready to use.

2) Remove outer leaves from heads of lettuce. Wash lettuce. Cut each head into 4 wedges, then 8.

3) Slice the tomatoes. Season with salt and pepper.

4) Peel the cooked, chilled hard-boiled eggs. Cut each egg in half.

5) Slice the onion into thin slices.

6) Alternate tomato and egg slices on serving plate. Place a lettuce wedge on each tomato. Top with sliced onion and Deviled Thousand Island Dressing.

7) Prepare Shrimp Corn Dogs.

8) Place 2 Shrimp Corn Dogs (tails-up) on each plate. Serve immediately.

SERVES 8

Shrimp Corn Dogs

INGREDIENTS

16 large (13-15 count) peeled, raw shrimp, tails intact

16 6-inch-long wooden skewers

½ cup flour

Canola oil for frying, as needed

METHOD

1) Prepare Kentucky Ale Batter, using recipe that follows (page 40).

2) Lay peeled shrimp out on cutting board. Cut 8-10 very shallow slits across the inner curve of the shrimp. Flip shrimp over and press down on the cutting board to straighten out.

3) Skewer each shrimp with a skewer from the tail side, stopping just before poking out the other end.

4) Preheat oven to 325 degrees Fahrenheit.

5) Also preheat to 325 degrees Fahrenheit a small table-top fryer or a 4-6-inch-tall, thick-bottomed pot with Canola oil, at least 3 inches deep.

6) Dust each skewered shrimp with the flour and then dip it into the batter, leaving the tail section of the shrimp uncovered. Shake off excess batter and place shrimp into the fryer in batches of 4, so as not to overload fryer. Cook each batch of shrimp for about 4-5 minutes. Remove from fryer and drain on paper towels, then store the fried shrimp on a baking sheet pan in the oven until the cooking process is complete.

7) Just prior to serving, grab each shrimp skewer and gently pull the skewer out about a centimeter to loosen it.

8) Serve immediately.

SERVES 8 (2 SHRIMP PER PERSON)

Kentucky Ale Batter

INGREDIENTS

4 egg whites, whipped
to soft peaks

2 12-ounce bottles of
Kentucky Ale, or other beer

3 tablespoons
vegetable oil

3 cups flour

1 ½ cups yellow cornmeal

1 teaspoon
cayenne powder

1 teaspoon onion powder

1 teaspoon garlic powder

3 tablespoons salt

¼ teaspoon baking powder

METHOD

1) Measure and sift all dry ingredients together.

2) Crack open 4 eggs and separate the egg whites. Whip these to a soft peak in a small stainless steel bowl. Set aside.

3) Combine beer and vegetable oil in a large mixing bowl. Stir in dry ingredients, just enough to blend. Fold in the whipped egg whites.

4) Store in a refrigerator until needed.

YIELDS ABOUT 6 CUPS

Deviled Thousand Island Dressing

INGREDIENTS

2 cups mayonnaise

3 ½ ounces Simple
Tomato Barbeque Sauce
(page 111)

2 tablespoons pickle relish

½ cup grated
hard-boiled eggs

¼ teaspoon
Dijon mustard

½ tablespoon
fine-diced yellow onion

¼ teaspoon
cayenne pepper

⅛ teaspoon salt

½ teaspoon
Worcestershire sauce

METHOD

1) Mix all ingredients together thoroughly.

2) Store in a refrigerator in an airtight container until needed.

3) Can be made up to 3 days ahead of time.

YIELDS 2 ½ CUPS

Kentucky Hot Slaw

INGREDIENTS

6 cups sliced green cabbage, ¼-inch thick

½ cup sliced red bell pepper, ¼-inch thick

½ cup sliced yellow bell pepper, ¼-inch thick

½ cup sliced green bell pepper, ¼-inch thick

½ cup sliced red onion, ¼-inch thick

¼ cup shredded carrots

2 cups Hot Slaw Dressing (page 44)

2 ounces vegetable oil

½ cup Pork Jowl Cracklings (page 45)

METHOD

1) In a large skillet or sauté pan, preheat oil, add cabbage, peppers, onion, and carrots and sauté for about 3-4 minutes, stirring often.

2) Pour in the Hot Slaw Dressing and simmer for about 5 minutes.

3) Add half the Pork Jowl Cracklings and stir.

4) Pour into serving dish and sprinkle with remaining Pork Jowl Cracklings.

SERVES 4

Hot Slaw Dressing

INGREDIENTS

1 ¾ cups cider vinegar

¼ cup Dijon mustard

¼ cup whole grain mustard

1 ½ cups brown sugar

1 ½ teaspoons salt

¼ teaspoon freshly-ground pepper

1 ½ cups reserved oil, from Pork Jowl Cracklings (page 45)

METHOD

1) Mix all ingredients together.

2) Can be made up to 1 week ahead of time and stored in a refrigerator. When refrigerated, the oil solidifies and separates from the other ingredients, so the dressing must be at room temperature at time of cooking to ensure proper proportions. Mix well before using.

YIELDS 4 CUPS

Pork Jowl Cracklings

INGREDIENTS

2 pounds whole smoked pork jowl (whole uncut slab bacon may be substituted)

Vegetable oil, as needed

Water, as needed

METHOD

1) Cut the pork into ½-inch cubes. Be sure to remove any rind from the pork.

2) Place the diced pork into a 4-6 inch-tall, thick-bottomed pot. Cover the pork with a half-and-half mixture of vegetable oil and water.

3) Place the pot over medium heat and allow the mixture to simmer for about 30 minutes, stirring every 5-10 minutes.

4) As the pork cooks, fat will be released from the pork and water will evaporate from the pan. When the water is almost all the way evaporated, the pork will start to darken and stick to the bottom of the pan. You will need to add approximately 1 cup of water and stir, but this should be done slowly so the oil will not boil over. Continue to simmer for another 30 minutes, stirring occasionally.

5) Repeat this process 1 more time, for a total cooking time of about 45 minutes. At the end of the last cooking step, do not add water. Remove pot from heat and carefully pour contents through a strainer over a metal bowl to catch the hot oil.

6) Dump the strained pork over paper towels to absorb excess grease. As the pork cools, it will become crispy. When cooled to room temperature, store in an airtight container. Cracklings can be stored for up to 1 week.

7) It is important to reserve cooking fat for the production of the hot slaw dressing.

YIELDS 1-2 CUPS

More than Burgoo

In Kentucky, burgoo is king. Its rich lore includes a Kentucky Derby winner, Burgoo King, who was named after the first man who made this concoction for 10,000 people. Its origin is credited to many; claimed by others. The ingredients list and consistency (soup or stew) is the subject of regional debate. In short, it is homebred, from the hollers to the hills. Kentucky burgoo reaches all the way back to frontier days and today it is the staple of political stump-jumps, church picnics, track kitchens and Southern gatherings.

At the end of the debate, it is a soup (or stew), created from what is at hand and open to the improvisation of the cook who makes it. With a few of my simple homemade stocks and your own imagination, soup can make a tempting beginning to any meal or a comforting family dinner.

With its legendary fertile soil and temperate climate, Kentucky supports more than 85,000 farms. Corn is one of Kentucky's largest cash crops and, during the late summer months, the abundance of sweet corn provides the inspiration for my Sweet Corn Chowder. I finish it off with Cornmeal-Fried Freshwater Shrimp.

Local mushrooms from Sheltowee Farm ("Sheltowee" was the Indian name given to Daniel Boone) grace my version of egg drop soup. Ribbons of egg are gently swirled into a mushroom fumet seasoned with sesame oil. Thinly-sliced scallions and shiitakes give texture.

My Black-Eyed Pea Chili is a regional take on the Southwestern classic. Kentucky bison and Southern black-eyed peas replace the usual beef and chili beans. A side of my Pimento Cheese Grit Fries makes this dish unbelievably good.

Ashland Estate – the home of Henry Clay – has always welcomed French inspiration. My vichyssoise (the chilled potato and leek soup credited to Chef Louis Diat of the Ritz-Carlton in New York City in the early 1900s) has a few new twists. It is finished with Capriole goat cheese and peppery Arugula Oil.

An addition of Buttermilk Whipped Cream enhances my Roasted Tomato Bisque, a pure Southern touch.

And, finally, my Kentucky Burgoo. I do keep the tradition of a variety of game meats and vegetables, but I skip the possum and squirrel and use locally-raised pork, beef and bison. Make my version or make it your own way, with a few personal twists. This remarkable Bluegrass dish should have a place at every family table.

MORE THAN BURGOO

Sweet Corn Chowder
with Cornmeal-Fried Freshwater Shrimp

Cornmeal-Fried Freshwater Shrimp

Kentucky Bison and Black-Eyed Pea Chili

Chilled Potato Vichyssoise
with Capriole Goat Cheese and Arugula Oil

Arugula Oil

Roasted Tomato Bisque with
Buttermilk Whipped Cream and Brioche Croutons

Buttermilk Whipped Cream
Brioche Croutons

Sheltowee Farm Shiitake Egg Drop Soup

Jonathan's Kentucky Burgoo

Chicken Stock

Shrimp Stock

Brown Beef Stock

Sweet Corn Chowder with Cornmeal-Fried Freshwater Shrimp

INGREDIENTS

12 fresh ears of corn, in the husk

Cool water to cover

2 tablespoons vegetable oil or bacon fat

2 cups small-diced yellow onion

2 cups small-diced celery

1 tablespoon chopped garlic

1 cup dry white wine

3 cups Shrimp Stock (page 60) (may substitute chicken or vegetable stock)

4 cups heavy cream

2 teaspoons sugar

¼ teaspoon ground cumin

¼ teaspoon turmeric

¼ teaspoon ground white pepper

1 tablespoon salt

1½ teaspoons sherry vinegar

METHOD

1) Preheat oven to 400 degrees Fahrenheit.

2) Place the fresh corn, still in the husk, on a cutting board, then use a large serrated knife to cut off the two ends. Feel the corn with your fingers and cut right where the kernels on the cob begin, discarding the scraps.

3) Place the corn in a large pot and cover with cool water. Allow the corn to soak for 15 minutes. Remove the corn from the water and place on a sheet tray. Roast corn in the oven for 15 minutes. Remove and allow it to cool.

4) Remove the husk from each ear of corn, being careful to remove the silks from the cob. Place one cob at a time on a cutting board, standing up, and slice off the kernels. Be careful when cutting. Do not cut too close to the cob, only about half-way into the kernel. This is done to keep the kernels small and tender. Then, using the backside of a knife, scrape or "milk" the cobs. Reserve the corn from the scraping process and store separately from the cut kernels. Discard the cobs.

5) In a medium-sized pot, preheat the oil on high heat. Sauté diced onions, celery and garlic for 2-3 minutes. De-glaze the pot with the white wine and simmer for 2 minutes to cook off alcohol.

6) Add remainder of ingredients and simmer on low heat for 20 minutes. Remove from heat and skim off any oil or foam from the top.

7) Serve Hot. May be stored in a refrigerator for up to 3 days.

YIELDS 3 CUPS - SERVES 10-12

Cornmeal-Fried Freshwater Shrimp

Freshwater shrimp farms have become popular in Kentucky over the past decade. The success of this new industry was made possible by research from Kentucky State University in the early 1990s. Shrimp are raised in aerated freshwater ponds, which are stocked in early June. Throughout the summer months, the farmers must regulate pH levels, fertilize, monitor feeding and control predators. In mid-September, ponds are drained and the shrimp are collected for sale. The majority of the harvest is consumed onsite or sold fresh at small farm festivals. If freshwater shrimp is not available, use any raw shrimp product available.

INGREDIENTS

18-20 medium-sized shrimp, peeled and de-veined

2 cups flour

5 eggs

1½ cups milk

4 cups yellow cornmeal

1 teaspoon garlic powder

1 teaspoon onion powder

2 teaspoons salt

1 teaspoon freshly-ground black pepper

½ teaspoon dried sage

1 teaspoon dried thyme

¼ teaspoon cayenne powder

1 cup vegetable oil

METHOD

1) Place flour in a medium-sized bowl. Set aside.

2) Mix eggs and milk together thoroughly. Set aside.

3) In a large mixing bowl, mix the remainder of the ingredients together. Set aside.

4) In a large skillet, preheat vegetable oil to 350 degrees Fahrenheit.

5) Dust the shrimp in the flour, one at a time. Dip the shrimp in the egg and milk mixture, then transfer into the cornmeal mixture. Repeat process until all shrimp are breaded in the cornmeal.

6) Place the shrimp in the skillet and sauté for about 2-3 minutes on each side. Remove from pan and place on a tray lined with paper towels. Repeat until all shrimp are cooked.

SERVES 6-8

Kentucky Bison and Black-Eyed Pea Chili

INGREDIENTS

1 cup dried
black-eyed peas

2 cups water

1 tablespoon vegetable oil

1 pound ground
bison or beef

1 cup small-diced
yellow onion

½ cup small-diced
green bell peppers

½ tablespoon
minced garlic

1 tablespoon paprika

1 tablespoon chili powder

½ teaspoon ground cumin

1 pinch ground cinnamon

1 cup Kentucky Ale, or
other beer of your choice

2 cups diced
canned tomatoes

2 cups tomato juice

½ tablespoon salt

1 teaspoon freshly-ground
black pepper

½ teaspoon puréed
chipotle peppers or half
of a jalapeño pepper,
chopped

METHOD

1) 3-4 hours before cooking chili, soak the 1 cup of dried black-eyed peas in 2 cups of water. Let them sit at room temperature until water has almost been absorbed into the peas.

2) Preheat the vegetable oil on high heat in a large soup pot.

3) Add ground meat and sauté for 3-4 minutes. Add onions, peppers and garlic. Continue to sauté another 3-4 minutes. Add paprika, chili powder, cumin and cinnamon.

4) Add beer and simmer for 2-3 minutes to allow alcohol to cook off.

5) Add tomatoes and tomato juice. Allow to come to a boil.

6) Reduce heat to a simmer and add the soaked black-eyed peas.

7) Simmer for about an hour or until black-eyed peas are fully cooked.

YIELDS 3 QUARTS · SERVES 8-12

Pairing notes: *Great by itself and even better served with Pimento Cheese Grit Fries*

Cooking notes: *Chili is always better on the second day. Store in a refrigerator and reheat later.*

Chilled Potato Vichyssoise with Capriole Goat Cheese and Arugula Oil

Vichyssoise is a French-inspired potato and leek soup. Its invention is credited to Chef Louis Diat of the Ritz-Carlton in New York City in the early 1900s. Here it is finished with goat cheese and peppery Arugula Oil.

INGREDIENTS

1 tablespoon vegetable oil

1 cup small-diced
yellow onions

1 cup small-diced celery

½ teaspoon minced garlic

½ cup dry white wine

5 cups peeled,
diced potatoes

½ tablespoon
fresh thyme leaves

2 cups heavy cream

6 cups Chicken Stock
(page 59) or broth

12 ounces goat cheese

1 tablespoon salt

½ teaspoon white pepper

Arugula Oil (page 54)

METHOD

1) In a large pot, preheat the vegetable oil on high heat. Add the onions, celery and garlic and sauté for 2-3 minutes.

2) Add white wine and reduce heat to a simmer. Cook for 3-4 minutes to cook off alcohol from the mixture.

3) Add potatoes, thyme, cream and Chicken Stock. Simmer for 12-15 minutes or until potatoes are tender. Remove from heat. Allow soup to cool to room temperature.

4) Place soup in a blender, along with the goat cheese, salt and white pepper. Purée until smooth.

5) Store in refrigerator.

6) At time of service, portion out chilled soup into bowls and drizzle 1 tablespoon of the Arugula Oil over the top of each portion of soup.

YIELDS ½ GALLON - SERVES 8

Arugula Oil

INGREDIENTS

1 cup olive oil

1 teaspoon salt

2 cups packed fresh arugula

METHOD

1) Place 1 cup olive oil in a medium-sized sauté pan, then place pan on high heat. When the oil becomes very hot, add the arugula and salt, then stir for about 20 seconds. Remove from heat, dump on a small sheet tray and quickly place in the refrigerator.

2) When thoroughly cooled, place the arugula and oil in a blender and purée until smooth. Pour contents of blender into a fine-mesh colander over a container to catch the green oil. Use a rubber spatula to help force Arugula Oil through the mesh. Discard the arugula solids from the colander. Store Arugula Oil in an airtight container in refrigerator until served. Use on the same day.

YIELDS 1 CUP

Roasted Tomato Bisque with Buttermilk Whipped Cream and Brioche Croutons

INGREDIENTS

8 cups quality canned whole tomatoes, drained and cut in half, reserving liquid

5 tablespoons brown sugar

2 teaspoons kosher salt

1 teaspoon freshly-ground black pepper

1 tablespoon chopped fresh thyme

3 tablespoons olive oil

1 cup diced yellow onion

1 cup diced celery

1 cup diced carrot

6 cloves of chopped garlic

1 cup dry white wine

5 cups tomato juice, reserved from canned tomatoes

2 bay leaves

1 tablespoon tomato paste

1 cup heavy cream

Buttermilk Whipped Cream (page 56)

Brioche Croutons (page 56)

METHOD

1) Preheat oven to 450 degrees Fahrenheit.

2) Drain whole tomatoes into a colander, over a bowl. Cut each tomato in half. Press down to squeeze excess liquid from the tomatoes. Reserve liquids for later use.

3) Place drained tomatoes on a sheet tray. Sprinkle tomatoes with brown sugar, salt, pepper and fresh thyme. Bake for about 12 minutes or just until slight browning and caramelization of brown sugar occurs. Remove from oven and allow tomatoes to cool.

4) In a medium-sized soup pot, preheat the olive oil on high heat. Add onions, celery and carrots and sauté for 2-3 minutes. Add garlic and sauté another 2-3 minutes. Deglaze pot with the white wine, then simmer for another 2-3 minutes to cook off alcohol. Add the reserved tomato juice, bay leaves and tomato paste. Simmer for 15 minutes on medium heat. Remove from heat and allow the soup base to cool.

5) Place the tomato soup base and the roasted tomatoes in a blender and purée until smooth. Pour into a clean soup pot and add heavy cream, then reheat for serving. This recipe can be made up to 3 days ahead of time and stored in a refrigerator.

6) Top each bowl of soup with a tablespoon of Buttermilk Whipped Cream and 3 or 4 Brioche Croutons.

YIELDS 3 QUARTS, OR 10-12 SERVINGS

Buttermilk Whipped Cream

INGREDIENTS

2 cups heavy cream

½ teaspoon salt

¼ teaspoon
ground white pepper

3 tablespoons buttermilk powder (found in the baking aisle in a grocery store)

METHOD

1) Place cream in a mixer with a whisk attachment.

2) Turn mixer on high speed. When cream starts to thicken, turn mixer off and add remaining ingredients, then turn mixer back on and continue to whip until cream comes to soft peaks.

3) Store in a refrigerator until needed. This recipe can be made a few hours before served.

YIELDS ABOUT 2 CUPS

Brioche Croutons

INGREDIENTS

4 cups ¼-inch cubed brioche bread, or you may substitute bread of choice

¼ cup melted butter

½ teaspoon salt

¼ teaspoon freshly-ground black pepper

METHOD

1) Preheat oven to 350 degrees Fahrenheit.

2) Place cubed bread in mixing bowl, then toss in melted butter, salt and pepper.

3) Lay out buttered bread cubes on sheet tray, then place in an oven and bake for about 10 minutes or until light tan and slightly crispy. Let cool. Store in an airtight container. Can be made up to 3 days ahead of time.

YIELDS 4 CUPS

Sheltowee Farm Shiitake Egg Drop Soup

INGREDIENTS

3 quarts Chicken Stock (page 59) or good quality canned chicken broth

6-8 dried, whole shiitake mushrooms

2 teaspoons freshly-grated ginger

1 tablespoon soy sauce

2 teaspoons sesame oil

1 tablespoon rice vinegar

2 tablespoons cornstarch

2 tablespoons cool water

4 eggs

1 cup thinly-sliced celery, cut on a bias

2 tablespoons finely-diced red bell peppers

4 cups thinly-sliced fresh shiitake mushrooms

Salt to taste

Freshly-ground black pepper to taste

1 cup grated carrot

1 cup thinly-sliced scallions

1 bunch fresh cilantro

METHOD

1) Place Chicken Stock in medium-sized soup pot. Add dried mushrooms, ginger, soy sauce, sesame oil and rice vinegar. Bring mixture to a boil, reduce heat and simmer for 15 minutes. Mix the cornstarch and cool water in a small bowl and stir into simmering soup. Continue to simmer the soup for 5 more minutes. Remove and discard mushrooms. Keep warm.

2) Crack open eggs into a small bowl. Whisk eggs until thoroughly mixed. While the soup pot is still simmering, slowly ribbon whisked eggs into hot soup, one tablespoon at a time, allowing each ribbon to rise from the bottom of the pot.

3) Carefully stir the celery, red peppers and fresh shiitakes into the soup, while trying not to break up the eggs too much. Continue to simmer soup gently for another 5 minutes. The soup is now ready to be served, or you may refrigerate it for up to 3 days, then gently reheat it.

4) At time of service, place 1 teaspoon of grated carrot, 1 teaspoon of scallions and a few cilantro leaves in each serving bowl, then ladle in hot soup.

YIELDS 3 QUARTS - SERVES 10-12

Jonathan's Kentucky Burgoo

INGREDIENTS

1 tablespoon olive oil

2 cups diced yellow onions

1 cup diced celery

1 cup peeled, diced carrots

½ cup diced green peppers

2 cups sliced shiitake mushrooms

½ tablespoon minced garlic

¼ teaspoon dried sage

½ teaspoon dried thyme

12-ounce bottle of Kentucky Ale or dark ale of your choice

½ gallon reserved bison braising liquid from Kentucky Bourbon Barrel Ale-Braised Bison Brisket (page 128) or Brown Beef Stock (page 61)

2 cups braised bison brisket, cut into bite-size pieces

2 cups roasted pork loin, cut into bite-size pieces

2 cups roasted beef tenderloin, cut into bite-size pieces

½ cup fresh roasted corn, cut off the cob

½ cup frozen soybeans – Edamame – or substitute lima beans or peas

¼ cup chopped canned tomatoes

Salt and fresh ground pepper to taste

METHOD

1) In a large soup pot, preheat the oil on high heat and sauté the onions, celery, carrots and peppers for 3-4 minutes.

2) Add the mushrooms, garlic and dried herbs. Sauté for 3-4 minutes more.

3) Add Kentucky Ale. Reduce heat to a simmer. Cook for about 5 minutes to allow alcohol to cook off.

4) Add remainder of ingredients and simmer for about 20 minutes before serving.

5) Can be made 2-3 days ahead of time and reheated.

SERVES 8-12

Pairing notes: *Served alone as an appetizer or topped off with some Crispy White Cheddar Grits as a luncheon or a light meal.*

Cooking notes: *Substitutions are encouraged in this recipe, but braising meat such as a brisket of beef or bison, top round or even a Boston pork butt will impart a tremendous amount of flavor to the soup.*

58

Chicken Stock

INGREDIENTS

10-12 pounds
chicken bones, backs,
necks, wings or 2 whole
4-5 pound roasting
chickens, well-rinsed.

1½ gallons cool water

2 medium yellow onions,
chopped

2 medium carrots,
chopped

4 stalks celery, chopped

1 leek, cut in half
and washed

8-10 cloves garlic

2 tablespoons black
peppercorns

5 bay leaves

1 cup white wine

1 bunch parsley stems,
chopped

METHOD

1) Place chicken bones in a large pot, cover with water and place on stove over high heat. Bring mixture to a boil, then skim off foam and fat that collect on top of stock.

2) Turn heat to low. Add remaining ingredients. Simmer about 1 hour, skimming as needed.

3) Remove from heat and allow stock to cool. Strain through a fine-mesh colander. Place stock in a clean pot and reduce to 1 gallon.

4) Store in refrigerator until needed. May be refrigerated for up to 1 week. Skim any hardened fat from top before reheating.

YIELDS 1 GALLON

Shrimp Stock

Purchase "shell on" shrimp and peel them yourself. Wrap the shells in plastic wrap and place in the freezer for later use.

INGREDIENTS

4-6 cups raw shrimp shells

2 medium yellow onions, diced

½ leek, well-washed to remove grit

1 celery stalk cut in ½-inch slices

1 medium-sized carrot, peeled and cut in ¼-inch slices

3 cloves garlic, smashed

2 bay leaves

2 teaspoons black peppercorns

3-4 sprigs fresh thyme

10 parsley stems

1-2 sprigs fresh dill

1 cup dry white wine

1 Roma tomato, sliced in half

1 teaspoon freshly-squeezed lemon juice

8 cups cool water

METHOD

1) Preheat oven to 400 degrees Fahrenheit.

2) Lay shrimp shells on a sheet tray and bake for 3-4 minutes. Remove from oven and mix the shells around to promote even cooking, then return them to the oven for another 3-4 minutes. Shells should turn bright pink and be slightly crispy. Remove and cool at room temperature. Pulse the shells in a food processor a few times to break down into small pieces.

3) Place all ingredients in stockpot. Place the pot over high heat and bring to a boil. Reduce heat to a simmer. Skim the surface to remove any foam.

4) Simmer stock for 30 minutes. Remove from heat and cool at room temperature.

5) Strain stock with a fine-mesh colander.

6) Place stock in a small pot and reduce to 1 quart.

7) Store in refrigerator for up to 3 days, until needed.

Y I E L D S   1   Q U A R T

Brown Beef Stock

INGREDIENTS

8 pounds veal bones

½ cup tomato paste

2 medium yellow onions, chopped

2 medium carrots, chopped

4 stalks celery

1 whole leek, cut in half lengthwise and well washed, to remove grit

8 cloves garlic, smashed

2 cups red wine

½ tablespoon dried thyme

4 bay leaves

2 tablespoons peppercorns

1 bunch parsley stems, chopped

2 gallons water

METHOD

1) Preheat oven to 450 degrees Fahrenheit.

2) Place the veal bones in a large roasting pan. Roast bones in the oven for about 20 minutes. Remove bones from the oven and flip them over. Return bones to the oven and roast another 20 minutes. Remove bones again, and smear tomato paste evenly over them. Return the bones to the oven and roast them another 20 minutes. Remove them from the oven and allow roasting pan to cool.

3) Transfer bones to a large stockpot.

4) Place roasting pan on stovetop over high heat and allow pan to become very hot, then deglaze the roasting pan with red wine. Scrape the bottom of the pan with a spatula to remove any burned pan drippings from the pan. Pour deglazing liquids into stockpot.

5) Add the remaining ingredients to the stockpot and simmer for about 3 hours on low heat. Skim the stock to remove excess fat. Strain through a colander and allow to cool. Discard bones and vegetables. Place stock in a clean pot and reduce liquid until 2 quarts remain.

6) Cool stock. Store in a refrigerator for up to 1 week. Remove any hardened fat before reheating.

YIELDS 2 QUARTS

Southern-Inspired Starters

Appetizers are my favorite part of any menu because they can be experimental and fun. Since appetizers are not the focal point of the meal, a new ingredient or a food with a strong flavor or too rich to be eaten in large quantities is usually met with a more open mind.

My Southern-Inspired Starters are intended to be provocative.

For my Country Ham Pot Stickers, I took the idea of the Asian dumpling and added the best country ham in Kentucky. The Colonel Bill Newsom Country Ham Company, which follows a recipe that has been handed down since the 1770s, produces hams in limited numbers, using an ambient weather cure and hickory smoke. My dumplings are steamed and then sautéed to produce a crispy bottom. They are served with Bourbon Soy and Peach Sweet-and-Sour Sauces.

My Sea Scallop Hot Brown is a riff on the classic Brown Hotel Hot Brown, featuring scallops, country ham, bacon and sliced tomatoes broiled with white cheddar cream sauce. Hot Browns have been a unique and luscious favorite at my restaurant for years.

Kentucky has more miles of waterways than any other state except Alaska. One of these waterways, Elkhorn Creek, where I played as a boy, provided water power for the historic Weisenburger Mill. I use their stone-ground grits to produce my Pimento Cheese Grit Fries.

First the grits are simmered with roasted peppers, white cheddar and cream, then I pour them onto a sheet pan to let them cool and become firm. These grits are cut into "fries," which are deep-fried to a crispy texture and served with Fire-Roasted Banana Pepper Mayonnaise and Green Tomato Piccalilli Relish.

My favorite crabmeat is King Crab. The flavor return is tremendous, but the prep, while simple, is time-consuming. So, make King Crab Cornbread Cakes on a weekend when other helpful hands are available, or when all little hands are at Grandma's. Pre-picked crabmeat of other varieties can be substituted, and dried cornbread breading is what makes these cakes truly special.

The precious wild blackberry, tiny and tart with wicked thorns, is still abundant, although their big hybrid cousin is most often what you see at the store. Look for our wild state fruit. The flavor is superior. During the late summer months of plenty, I simmer them into wonderful blackberry preserves, perfect with Seared Foie Gras and old-fashioned Beaten Biscuits.

Two southern home favorites get a new twist with my recipes for Traditional Deviled Eggs and Kentucky Bourbon Barrel Ale Beer Cheese. And my Mushrooms and Dumplings, Redneck Rockefellers, Potato-Spun Shrimp and Pepper-Seared Beef Carpaccio are all about twist. I did promise provocative.

SOUTHERN-INSPIRED STARTERS

Pimento Cheese Grit Fries

Green Tomato Piccalilli Relish
Fire-Roasted Banana Pepper Mayonnaise
Fire-Roasted Banana Pepper Purée

Deviled Egg Trio

Smoked Salmon
Country Ham
Asparagus-Chive

Traditional Deviled Eggs

Mushrooms and Dumplings

Potato-Parmesan Dumplings
Browned Butter
Caramelized Onions

King Crab Cornbread Cakes

Roasted Corn Aioli

Country Ham Pot Stickers

Bourbon Soy Dipping Sauce
Peach Sweet-and-Sour Sauce

Kentucky Bourbon Barrel Ale Beer Cheese

Redneck Rockefellers

Jonathan's Pimento Cheese

Sea Scallop Hot Browns

Sea Scallop Hot Brown Sauce

Seared Foie Gras

Blackberry Balsamic Preserves

Potato-Spun Shrimp

Pepper-Seared Beef Carpaccio

Roasted Garlic Oil

Pimento Cheese Grit Fries

This dish was inspired by French fries and mayonnaise. I blend in a few Southern touches, such as banana peppers, pimento cheese, grits and green tomatoes. These grit fries are truly a one-of-a-kind dish.

INGREDIENTS

2 cups puréed roasted pimento peppers, canned

2 ½ cups heavy cream

5 cups water

2½ cups grits, not instant style

1 cup shredded white cheddar cheese

1 teaspoon salt

1 teaspoon white pepper

1 teaspoon cayenne pepper

Oil for frying

Green Tomato Piccallili Relish (page 68)

Fire-Roasted Banana Pepper Mayonnaise (page 69)

METHOD

1) Mix together pepper purée, heavy cream and water in a medium-sized pot and place over high heat. Bring to a boil.

2) Stir in the grits until thoroughly incorporated.

3) Reduce heat to low, just enough to simmer. Continue to cook for approximately 20 minutes, stirring often.

4) Stir in cheddar cheese, salt, white pepper and cayenne pepper. Continue to simmer another 10 minutes.

5) Remove from heat and pour grits onto a greased cookie sheet pan.

6) Refrigerate for 2 hours.

7) When thoroughly firm, flip pan over onto a cutting board.

8) Cut the grits into ½-inch thick bars approximately 3 inches long.

9) Place the "fries" onto another cookie sheet pan lined with parchment paper and place in the freezer.

10) When ready to serve, place about ¾ inch of oil into a large skillet. Heat the oil to 350 degrees Fahrenheit, then place the grit fries into the skillet. Allow the fries to develop a golden color with a crispy texture.

11) Remove the fries from the pan and place them on paper towels to absorb excess oil.

12) Line a plate with Fire-Roasted Banana Pepper Mayonnaise. Stack Grit Fries (5 per plate) like Lincoln Logs and top each stack with 1-2 tablespoons of Green Tomato Piccallili Relish.

MAKES ABOUT 50 FRIES - SERVES 6 (8 FRIES EACH)

Pairing notes: Pimento Cheese Grit Fries with Fire-Roasted Banana Pepper Mayonnaise and Green Tomato Piccalilli Relish. Bison and Black-Eyed Pea Chili with Pimento Cheese Grit Fries.

Cooking notes: Grit Fries can be prepared, cut and frozen for up to 24 hours. The final frying process should be done at the time of serving.

Green Tomato Piccalilli Relish

This Green Tomato Piccalilli Relish offers a sweet and sour burst of flavors that is an excellent accompaniment to fish, pork or shrimp.

INGREDIENTS

3 cups diced
green tomatoes

1 cup diced yellow onion

1 cup diced red pepper

1 cup diced green pepper

1 cup diced yellow pepper

1 ½ cups cider vinegar

1 ¾ cups sugar

1 tablespoon salt

½ teaspoon ground allspice

1 cinnamon stick

2 tablespoons
mustard seeds

½ tablespoon celery seeds

1 bay leaf

METHOD

1) Dice green tomatoes, onions, and bell peppers into ¼-inch cubes.

2) Place diced vegetables and 1 cup of the cider vinegar into a medium-sized pot and place over high heat. Bring to a boil. Reduce heat to low and simmer for 20 minutes, stirring often. Remove from heat and drain vegetables in colander. Discard liquid.

3) Return drained vegetables back to the pot. Add remaining ingredients. Return to high heat and boil for 3 minutes. Remove from heat and allow mixture to cool.

4) Store in a refrigerator up to 2 weeks.

YIELDS 7 CUPS

Pairing notes: *Pimento Cheese Grit Fries with Green Tomato Piccalilli and Fire-Roasted Banana Pepper Mayonnaise.*

Cooking notes: *Best when made a few days ahead of time to allow flavors to blend together. Piccalilli can be stored in the refrigerator for up to 2 weeks. Remove cinnamon stick and bay leaf before serving.*

Fire-Roasted Banana Pepper Mayonnaise

INGREDIENTS

1 cup mayonnaise

6 tablespoons Fire-Roasted Banana Pepper Purée (recipe below)

½ teaspoon salt

⅛ teaspoon white pepper

⅛ teaspoon cayenne powder (only after you have tasted the finished product)

METHOD

1) Mix all ingredients in a small bowl and stir together thoroughly.
2) Can be made up to 2 days ahead of time. Store, covered, in a refrigerator.

YIELDS 1 CUP

Fire-Roasted Banana Pepper Purée

INGREDIENTS

6-8 fresh banana peppers (Use yellow peppers, not green.)

2 yellow bell peppers

1 tablespoon Dijon mustard

1 tablespoon freshly-squeezed lemon juice

METHOD

1) Place the peppers on a grill or over an open flame from a gas burner. Lightly char peppers. Remove from grill and place in a small bowl covered with plastic wrap.
2) When cool, peel skin from the peppers.
3) Remove seeds. (You may want to use rubber gloves while removing seeds. Banana peppers can be spicy and handling the seeds can cause skin irritation.)
4) Place all ingredients in the bowl of a food processor and purée until smooth.
5) Stop machine a few times to scrape down sides and restart. This is done to ensure mixture is puréed thoroughly.
6) Can be made up to 2 days ahead of time or frozen in ice trays for future use.

YIELDS ½ CUP

Deviled Egg Trio

SMOKED SALMON

INGREDIENTS

1 cup traditional deviled egg filling, ⅓ of the filling from Tradtional Deviled Egg recipe (page 72)

4 tablespoons smoked salmon, very finely-diced

1 teaspoon chopped fresh dill

Salmon caviar, as a garnish

METHOD

1) Follow traditional deviled egg recipe. Divide egg yolk filling into 3 equal parts to complete trio.

2) Mix filling with smoked salmon and chopped dill.

3) Load mixture into a pastry bag with no tip. Pipe the filling into 12 egg white halves.

4) Garnish each egg with salmon caviar and a small fresh dill sprig.

5) Store in an airtight container in the refrigerator for up to 1 day

YIELDS 12

COUNTRY HAM

INGREDIENTS

1 cup traditional deviled egg filling, ⅓ of the filling from Tradtional Deviled Egg recipe (page 72)

5 tablespoons finely-diced country ham

METHOD

1) Follow traditional deviled egg recipe. Divide egg yolk filling into 3 equal parts to complete trio.

2) Mix filling with 4 tablespoons of the chopped country ham.

3) Load mixture into a pastry bag with no tip. Pipe the filling into 12 egg white halves.

4) Garnish each egg with a pinch of the remaining 1 tablespoon of chopped country ham.

5) Store in an airtight container in the refrigerator for up to 1 day.

YIELDS 12

ASPARAGUS-CHIVE

INGREDIENTS

1 cup traditional deviled egg filling, ⅓ of the filling from Tradtional Deviled Egg recipe (page 72)

3 tablespoons blanched chilled asparagus, very finely diced

2 tablespoons chives or scallions, very finely diced

METHOD

1) Follow traditional deviled egg recipe. Divide egg yolk filling into 3 equal parts to complete trio.

2) Mix filling with asparagus and chives.

3) Load mixture into a pastry bag with no tip. Pipe the filling into 12 egg white halves.

4) Garnish each egg with an inch-long blanched asparagus tip that has been sliced in half lengthwise.

5) Store in an airtight container in the refrigerator for up to 1 day.

YIELDS 12

Traditional Deviled Eggs

INGREDIENTS

24 whole eggs

½ gallon cool water

2 tablespoons salt

2 cups vinegar

2 cups cooked egg yolks

1 tablespoon pickle relish

1 tablespoon Dijon mustard

1 teaspoon kosher salt

1 teaspoon cayenne pepper

1 cup mayonnaise

As needed: paprika to garnish

METHOD

1) Place water, salt and vinegar into a large pot with a lid and bring to a full rolling boil. Carefully drop 1 egg at a time into the boiling water. Return pot lid, and when water is back to a full rolling boil. Allow eggs to boil for 10-12 minutes. Remove from heat and pour off most of the water. Put the remaining eggs and water into a large bowl half full of ice.

2) When the eggs are cool to the touch, crack and remove the shells. Store peeled eggs in a bowl of cool water.

3) Place 1 egg at a time on a cutting board. Hold the egg on the cutting board with the long side pointing toward the top and bottom of the cutting board. Using a sharp paring knife, slice a very small piece off each egg on both the left and right sides to provide the deviled egg with a small flat base so the egg can be stable when filling and serving.

4) Cut each egg in half between the 2 flat bases. Remove yolks and place into a measuring cup to measure out the needed 2 cups of cooked egg yolks. Place the cooked egg white shells in a small bowl filled halfway with cool water. When all whites have been added to the bowl, mix them around in the water to wash away any remaining yolk. Pour off water and repeat process. Store whites in cool, clean water while making the fillings.

5) Place the needed 2 cups of yolks into a food processor with pickle relish, Dijon mustard, salt and cayenne pepper. Purée mixture to a smooth consistency, stop machine and scrape down sides. Then purée again to achieve a thoroughly smooth consistency. Stop the processor, add the mayonnaise and purée again. You may need to stop and scrape down the sides of the processor a few times to make sure you have a thoroughly smooth and blended mixture. Store in a refrigerator for at least 1 hour for the mixture to set to the proper consistency.

6) Remove the egg white halves from the water bath. Place each egg upside down over paper towels to drain. Transfer 36 of the egg white halves onto a sheet pan and turn them right side up. Some egg whites may be damaged and are less than perfect. You may even have a few extra.

7) Load the egg yolk filling into a pastry bag with a medium-sized star tip. Pipe a generous amount of the filling into each egg with a slight circular motion. When shell is filled, stop applying pressure to the pastry bag and then lift up.

8) Garnish the top of each deviled egg with a small pinch of paprika.

9) Store in an airtight container in a refrigerator. May be made up to 1 day in advance.

YIELDS 36

Mushrooms and Dumplings

INGREDIENTS

2 tablespoons olive oil

1 tablespoon chopped fresh garlic

4 cups sliced mushrooms (shiitakes are best)

½ cup white wine

1½ cups vegetable stock or Chicken Stock (page 59)

12-16 Potato-Parmesan Dumplings (page 74)

½ cup Caramelized Onions (page 75)

¼ cup heavy cream

2 teaspoons salt

1 teaspoon freshly-ground black pepper

4 tablespoons chilled Browned Butter (page 75)

4 tablespoons chopped fresh flat leaf parsley

METHOD

1) Preheat olive oil in a large sauté pan. Add garlic and sauté for about 1 minute. Add mushrooms and continue to sauté for another 2 minutes.

2) De-glaze pan with white wine and stock. Add dumplings, onions, cream, salt and pepper. Simmer mixture for about 6-8 minutes.

3) Remove from heat. Add parsley and Browned Butter, while gently stirring, until chilled butter has melted.

4) Place 3-4 dumplings on each serving plate, top each off with mushrooms, onions and pan sauce.

SERVES 4

Potato-Parmesan Dumplings

INGREDIENTS

5 medium Idaho potatoes

3 cups flour

3 tablespoons heavy cream

1 tablespoon kosher salt

3 whole eggs

1 ⅓ cups finely-grated, good quality Parmesan cheese

METHOD

1) Peel and dice potatoes into 1-inch cubes. Place in a medium-sized pot, cover with cool water and bring to a boil over high heat. Cook potatoes about 10 minutes or until tender. Dump potatoes in a colander and allow them to cool.

2) Using a potato ricer or a drum sieve, process the potatoes to a smooth, lump-free consistency. Measure out 1⅔ cups riced potatoes. There will likely be leftover cooked potatoes after you measure the 1⅔ cups of riced potatoes needed. They can be saved and used for something else or discarded.

3) Place all ingredients in a mixer with dough hook attachment and mix for about 3-4 minutes. Transfer the dough to a floured work surface, cover with plastic wrap and let rest for about 10 minutes.

4) Roll out the dough with a rolling pin to about ¼-inch thick. Cut into desired shape. A small diamond, cut about 1 inch long, works well.

5) Bring a large pot of salted water to a boil on high heat. Carefully drop the dumplings into the boiling water while stirring gently. Boil dumplings for 10 minutes, drain into a colander and rinse with cool water.

6) When the dumplings are cool to the touch, transfer to a storage container and cover with cool water.

7) Store cooked dumplings in a refrigerator until needed. May be made up to 3 days ahead of time.

SERVES 6

Browned Butter

INGREDIENTS

1 pound butter

2 cups heavy cream

METHOD

1) Place butter and cream in a small pot over medium heat.

2) Simmer mixture, stirring often, for about 10 minutes or until the butter solids start to turn a light tan color and give off a toasty aroma.

3) Pour browned butter from the pot into a shallow baking dish and place in a refrigerator to cool.

4) When the brown butter is starting to set, stir to thoroughly mix, then return to refrigerator.

5) When totally set, the Browned Butter can be cut into cubes.

Caramelized Onions

INGREDIENTS

1 medium-sized yellow onion

2 tablespoons olive oil

6-8 tablespoons water, as needed

METHOD

1) Slice onions into ¼-inch slices.

2) Add onions and olive oil to a medium-sized sauté pan. Place the pan over low heat and cover. Gently sauté onions for about 5 minutes, stirring occasionally.

3) When the onions start to lightly brown and the pan starts to dry, add 2 tablespoons of water to the pan. This is done to allow the onions to caramelize and not burn. When the pan dries again, add 2 more tablespoons. Continue this process until the onions are soft and caramelized.

4) Remove from heat and store in a refrigerator until needed. Onions can be caramelized up to 3 days ahead of time.

YIELDS ABOUT 1 ¼ CUPS

King Crab Cornbread Cakes

Crab cakes are a very popular way to enjoy crabmeat and are prepared in countless ways. This recipe is special because of the use of dried cornbread for the breading base of the cakes. There are many varieties of crab from which to choose. My favorite type is King Crab legs, usually purchased pre-cooked and frozen. This is not the cheapest crab product, and it is time-consuming to remove the meat from the shell, but it is delicious. Prepare the crabmeat by submerging the crab in salted boiling water for about 5 minutes, then remove crab from the water and allow it to cool. When the crab is cool enough to handle, break down the legs and remove the meat.

INGREDIENTS

2 whole eggs

2 cups dried cornbread crumbs

½ cup dried breadcrumbs (Panko or crushed crackers can also be used)

1 tablespoon vegetable oil

¾ cup small-diced yellow onions

½ cup small-diced celery

¼ cup small-diced red bell peppers

1 teaspoon minced garlic

¼ cup white wine

1 teaspoon Dijon mustard

1¼ pounds cooked King Crab meat, picked from the shell

⅓ cup mayonnaise

1 teaspoon salt

½ teaspoon freshly-ground black pepper

½ cup cornmeal

⅓ cup vegetable oil

METHOD

1) Place cornbread, breadcrumbs and eggs into a large mixing bowl and mix well. Set aside.

2) In a large sauté pan, preheat vegetable oil on high heat. When hot, sauté the onions, celery, pepper and garlic until the vegetables are tender. Add white wine and continue to cook until the alcohol is cooked out of the mixture, about 3-4 minutes. There should still be some liquid remaining in the pan. Set aside to cool.

3) Add all ingredients except cornmeal and vegetable oil to the breadcrumb and egg mixture. Mix well until fully incorporated. Divide crab cakes into 8 equal portions. This step can be done up to a day in advance.

4) At the time of serving, dust the cakes in cornmeal, then preheat a large sauté pan with ⅓ cup vegetable oil on high heat. Sauté the cakes on both sides for about 3-4 minutes each to develop a golden brown color.

5) Remove cakes from pan and place on a plate lined with paper towels to absorb any excess oil. Plate and serve.

SERVES 4 (8 2½-OUNCE CAKES)

Pairing notes: *King Crab Cornbread Cakes with arugula and Roasted Corn Aioli. The crab cakes are great as a sandwich or as an entrée.*

Cooking notes: *Other types of crab can be substituted. The cornbread can also be substituted for regular breadcrumbs.*

Roasted Corn Aioli

INGREDIENTS

4 coddled egg yolks
(see cooking notes below)

2 cups roasted yellow corn, cut from the cob

1 tablespoon minced garlic

½ teaspoon Dijon mustard

1 teaspoon freshly-squeezed lemon juice

½ teaspoon ground cumin

½ teaspoon salt

¼ teaspoon ground white pepper

2 cups olive oil

METHOD

1) In a medium-sized pot, bring 2 quarts of water to a boil. Carefully place 4 whole eggs into the water. Boil the eggs for 2 minutes. Remove eggs from water. Place eggs on a tray and cool in the refrigerator.

2) Once the eggs are fully cooled, crack them open and remove and save the yolks only. Discard the shells and the whites. Place the yolks into the refrigerator for up to 1 hour before making the aioli.

3) Place 8-10 ears of fresh corn still in the husk on a cutting board, then use a large serrated knife to cut 1 inch off each end. Feel the corn with your fingers and cut right where the kernels on the cob begin, discarding the scraps.

4) Place the corn in a large pot, cover it with cool water and let it soak for 20 minutes. Remove the corn from the water and place it on a sheet tray.

5) Roast corn in a 400-degree Fahrenheit oven for 20 minutes. Remove and allow corn to cool.

6) Cut the corn from the cob. Reserve any leftover corn to garnish final plate.

7) Place all ingredients in food processor, except for the olive oil, and purée until smooth.

8) With machine still running slowly, add the olive oil to form an emulsion.

9) Store in refrigerator until needed. The Aioli should be consumed the day it is made.

YIELDS 4 CUPS

Pairing notes: *King Crab Cornbread Cakes with Roasted Corn Aioli*

Cooking notes: *The eggs and part of the whites will be cooked. The yolk should still be runny. The coddling process is done to reduce the risk of food-borne illness associated with consuming raw egg yolks. The recipe calls for 4 coddled egg yolks, but I suggest you coddle 6. It is a good idea to have extra in case of damage or imperfections. This step will ensure that you will not have to repeat the process to finish the recipe.*

Country Ham Pot Stickers

Many just love Chinese-style dumplings. In this interpretation, I use country ham and pair the dumplings with two Southern-inspired dipping sauces.

INGREDIENTS

1 tablespoon vegetable oil

½ pound diced country ham

½ cup small-diced yellow onions

¼ cup thinly-sliced celery

1 cup diced green cabbage

1 teaspoon grated fresh ginger

½ teaspoon minced garlic

1 tablespoon shredded carrots

1 tablespoon chopped parsley

5 7 x 7-inch square egg roll wrappers, cut into fourths

A small dish of warm water

3 tablespoons vegetable oil

METHOD

1) In a large sauté pan, preheat the vegetable oil on high heat.
2) Add the country ham and sauté for 2 minutes. Add onions, celery, cabbage, garlic, carrots and parsley. Continue to sauté for another 3- 4 minutes until vegetables are tender. Remove from heat.
3) Place mixture in a food processor and pulse the machine until it is coarsley ground. Store in a refrigerator for 20-30 minutes.
4) Using a tablespoon, portion mix into 18-20 balls.
5) Place 1 of the filling balls into the middle of each 3 ½-inch-square egg roll wrapper.
6) Fold wrapper in half horizontally, with the triangle pointing up.
7) Hold the top of the triangle with left hand. Use your right hand to dip your finger into warm water. Moisten the seams.
8) Still holding top with left hand, use your right hand to grab the halfway mark on the right-hand seam and fold this seam toward the top. Make 3 to 4 pleats, moving toward the top until the bottom right point reaches the top.
9) Still holding in your left hand, rotate dumpling. Dip your right index finger into water dish and moisten the inside seam on the right hand side. Press to seal.
10) Repeat process. This is difficult at first, but you will get the hang of it.
11) Using a basket steamer, steam dumplings for about 5 minutes.
12) In a large non-stick sauté pan, preheat 3 tablespoons of vegetable oil on medium heat. Place dumplings bottom-side-down in pan and sauté until bottoms turn light brown and crispy. Remove and serve.

YIELDS ABOUT 2½ CUPS, OR 18-20 DUMPLINGS

Pairing notes: Country Ham Pot Stickers with Peach Sweet-and-Sour and Bourbon Soy Dipping Sauces

Cooking notes: Pot stickers can be steamed and stored covered in a refrigerator up to 2 days ahead of time. At time of serving, the dumplings can be re-steamed to heat insides, then sautéed.

Bourbon Soy Dipping Sauce

This simple sauce puts a Kentucky twist on an Asian-style dipping sauce.

INGREDIENTS

7 ounces good quality soy sauce

1 ounce Bourbon

1 teaspoon sesame oil

1 tablespoon thinly-sliced chives or scallions

METHOD

1) Mix all ingredients together.
2) Can be made up to 2 weeks ahead of time, but keep refrigerated.

YIELDS 1 CUP

Peach Sweet-and-Sour Sauce

This simple sweet-and-sour sauce was developed to accompany the Country Ham Pot Stickers. You can use my fresh peach preserves with this recipe or you can purchase pre-made preserves.

INGREDIENTS

1½ cups Peach Preserves (page 23) or store-bought product

½ cup cider vinegar

METHOD

1) Place ingredients in a blender and purée.
2) May be made ahead of time and stored in a refrigerator for up to 2 weeks.

YIELDS 2 CUPS

Kentucky Bourbon Barrel Ale Beer Cheese

Beer cheese has become a Kentucky tradition – standard during the holidays, at Derby parties and other social gatherings. Kentucky Bourbon Barrel Ale adds a one-of-a-kind flavor to this traditional Kentucky favorite. Serve with carrots, celery and assorted crackers. Other interesting ways to use this beer cheese is as a topping for grilled burgers and to flavor stone-ground grits.

INGREDIENTS

14 ounces sharp yellow cheddar cheese

4 ounces smoked cheddar cheese

8 ounces cream cheese, softened

2 tablespoons Caramelized Onions (page 75)

12-ounce bottle of Kentucky Bourbon Barrel Ale

1 tablespoon Bourbon

¼ teaspoon freshly-ground black pepper

½ teaspoon salt

½ teaspoon onion powder

½ teaspoon garlic powder

2 tablespoons paprika

¼ teaspoon cayenne powder

METHOD

1) Use a box grater to shred the yellow and smoked cheddar cheese.

2) In a food processor, purée the onions, shredded cheeses and Caramelized Onions.

3) With the processor running, slowly add the beer.

4) Stop the processor and scrape down the sides. Turn the machine back on. Repeat, as needed, to produce a smooth consistency.

5) Add the remaining ingredients and continue to purée. Repeat the scraping process, as needed, to ensure a creamy smooth consistency.

6) Store in the refrigerator until serving. In fact, it is best to make this a few days ahead of time to allow for the flavors to develop and to allow the mixture to set. Can be stored in the refrigerator for up to 2 weeks.

YIELDS ABOUT 3 CUPS

Pairing notes: Serve with cornbread, crackers and crudités, or as a topping for grilled burgers.

Kentucky Ale and **Kentucky Bourbon Barrel Ale** are trademarked products of the Alltech Lexington Brewing and Distilling Co., Lexington, Kentucky.

Redneck Rockefellers

Baked oysters can be served in countless ways, but the most famous dish is Oysters Rockefeller. This recipe embraces the traditional, but is given a Kentucky twist by using ingredients from close to home. Most of all, I love the name of my version.

INGREDIENTS

12 fresh oysters

1 tablespoon olive oil

½ small-diced yellow onion

½ pound fresh spinach

1 teaspoon salt

½ teaspoon freshly-ground black pepper

1 cup Jonathan's Pimento Cheese (recipe below)

¼ pound cooked country ham, diced

METHOD

1) Preheat oven to 400 degrees Fahrenheit.
2) Wash oysters in cool water. Pry open with oyster shucker. Discard top shell. Set aside.
3) Preheat sauté pan with olive oil and sauté onions for about 2 minutes. Add spinach and sauté, just till spinach is tender. Season with salt and pepper. Remove from heat and set aside.
4) Place about 1 tablespoon spinach and onions over each oyster.
5) Place about 2 teaspoons Jonathan's Pimento Cheese over each oyster.
6) Place 1 teaspoon diced country ham over each oyster
7) Bake oysters for about 8-10 minutes, or until thoroughly warmed and slightly browned on top.

SERVES 6

Jonathan's Pimento Cheese

INGREDIENTS

2 red bell peppers, whole

1 yellow bell pepper, whole

2 tablespoons vegetable oil

6 cups white cheddar cheese, thickly-grated

1 ½ cups mayonnaise

1 teaspoon salt

¼ teaspoon ground white pepper

METHOD

1) Preheat oven to 400 degrees Fahrenheit.
2) In a medium-sized bowl, toss the whole bell peppers with the vegetable oil.
3) Place peppers on a baking sheet tray and roast in the oven for about 8 minutes. Flip peppers a few times during the roasting process to ensure even cooking
4) Remove from oven. Place back in a bowl and cover with plastic wrap. Allow peppers to cool at room temperature.
5) Place peppers on a cutting board and remove the skins from the peppers. They should be easily removed. If they prove difficult to remove, place the peppers back in the oven for a few more minutes, then return them to the bowl and cover them with plastic wrap again.
6) Cut peppers open and remove seeds.
7) Roughly chop the bell peppers.
8) Mix all ingredients into a large mixing bowl.
9) Refrigerate until needed. May be stored up to 3 days.

YIELDS 6 CUPS

Sea Scallop Hot Browns

INGREDIENTS

4 cups water

1 teaspoon salt

6 large fresh sea scallops

3 strips sliced bacon

1 loaf unsliced brioche bread. (May substitute sourdough loaf or baguette)

¼ pound thinly-sliced cooked country ham

4 cups Sea Scallop Hot Brown Sauce (page 89)

12 cherry tomatoes

METHOD

1) In a small pot, bring the water and salt to a boil. Submerge scallops into boiling water and stir. Allow to cook for about 3 minutes. Remove from heat and dump about 6 cups of ice into pot to stop the cooking process. Allow to cool. Drain off water. Cut each scallop in half horizontally. Set aside.

2) Preheat oven to 350 degrees Fahrenheit.

3) Lay the bacon out on a sheet tray and place in oven. Bake for about 5-7 minutes to halfway cook the bacon. Remove and allow it to cool to room temperature. Cut bacon into 2 ½-inch slices. Take each of the 2 ½-inch bacon slices and slice into 3 ribbons.

4) Slice bread into 1-inch-thick slices. Using a 3-inch ring mold or biscuit cutter, press out 12 bread rounds. If a small circular cutter is unavailable, cut the bread into 3-inch squares. Place bread on a sheet tray and toast in the oven. Remove and let cool at room temperature.

5) Press small indentions into top of toasted bread rounds with your finger. Scoop about a teaspoon of the chilled Sea Scallop Hot Brown Sauce on top of each piece of the toasted bread. Lay 2 slices of country ham on each, cut to the same size as the bread. Next lay 1 slice of the par-cooked sea scallops on each. Scoop out another teaspoon of the chilled Sea Scallop Hot Brown Sauce over each scallop. Lay 2 of the bacon ribbons in an "X" over each scallop.

6) Refrigerate until ready to cook. The Sea Scallop Hot Browns can be prepped to this point up to a day before being served.

7) Preheat oven to 400 degrees Fahrenheit.

8) Slice the cherry tomatoes into thin slices, about 3 per tomato.

9) In a small pot, reheat the remaining sauce over low heat, stirring often.

10) Place Sea Scallop Hot Browns on a sheet tray and bake for about 6 minutes, or until thoroughly warmed. Remove from oven and place on a serving tray or individual plates lined with a little of the warmed sauce. Top off each of the Sea Scallop Hot Browns with a cherry tomato slice.

S E R V E S   4   (3   P E R   P E R S O N)

Sea Scallop Hot Brown Sauce

INGREDIENTS

3 ounces butter

4 tablespoons flour

2 cups heavy cream

2 cups Shrimp Stock
(page 60) (May substitute
store-purchased clam juice)

2 cups shredded white
cheddar cheese

1 teaspoon salt

¼ teaspoon ground
white pepper

METHOD

1) Make a roux by melting the butter in a small sauté pan, stirring in flour and cooking over low heat for about 5 minutes, stirring often. Remove from heat and set aside for later use.

2) Place the cream and Shrimp Stock into a small pot and bring to a boil. Stir in grated cheddar cheese. Stir until melted.

3) Pour about a third of the cream mixture into a small stainless steel bowl and whisk in about 3 tablespoons of roux. Stir the mixture until it becomes thick and smooth.

4) Pour roux mixture back into the pot with the rest of the cream and whisk until smooth. Allow mixture to simmer for about 5 minutes to finish cooking and to thicken.

5) Remove from heat and refrigerate. This step is best done a few hours before production of the Sea Scallop Hot Browns. May be made up to 3 days in advance.

YIELDS 4 CUPS

Seared Foie Gras

INGREDIENTS

12 (each 1-1½ ounces) foie gras medallions, cut about ¼-inch thick and 2 inches wide

1 tablespoon salt

1 teaspoon freshly-ground black pepper

½ cup Blackberry Balsamic Preserves (recipe below)

12 Beaten Biscuits (page 168)

METHOD

1) Preheat a large sauté pan on high heat.

2) Place foie gras medallions in hot sauté pan and sauté each side for about 1 minute. Be careful not to over-cook foie gras. Season with salt and pepper.

3) Remove from pan and serve over the Beaten Biscuits with Blackberry Balsamic Preserves.

SERVES 12

Pairing notes: *Seared Foie Gras with Blackberry Balsamic Preserves on Beaten Biscuits.*

Blackberry Balsamic Preserves

INGREDIENTS

4 cups packed fresh blackberries

1 teaspoon fresh lemon juice

1 cup balsamic vinegar

1 box (1.75 oz.) Sure-Jell fruit pectin

7 cups sugar

METHOD

1) Crush berries into a quart-size measuring cup.

2) Squeeze out 1 teaspoon fresh lemon juice over berries.

3) Measure out 1 cup balsamic vinegar.

4) Place berries, lemon juice, balsamic vinegar and fruit pectin in a medium-sized sauce pot.

5) Bring mixture to a full rolling boil.

6) Whisk in the 7 cups of sugar. Continue to stir until a full rolling boil is achieved again, and allow preserves to boil for 1 full minute.

7) Remove from heat and cool at room temperature.

8) Can be strained through a fine-mesh strainer at this point if you would like to remove seeds.

9) Store in refrigerator for up to 2 weeks.

YIELDS 5 CUPS

Potato-Spun Shrimp

INGREDIENTS

12 large peeled shrimp

5-6 large Idaho potatoes

2 tablespoons kosher salt

1 teaspoon freshly-ground black pepper

2 cups flour

Vegetable oil, as needed

METHOD

1) Preheat at least 3 inches of vegetable oil in a fryer or large heavy pot to 325 degrees Fahrenheit.

2) Place flour on a large plate on a work surface.

3) Sprinkle shrimp with salt and pepper.

4) Cut about ½ inch off each side of the potatoes.

5) Work with 1 potato at a time. Place a potato on the Japanese mandolin and spin to produce the potato threads. Use your hand to gather the long thread of potato in a bundle, allowing short thread to fall on the table. Only wrap shrimp with long potato threads.

6) Carefully wrap 2-4 shrimp with the thread accumulated from 1 potato. Set aside and repeat process.

7) When all shrimp have been wrapped, blanch-fry the shrimp in small batches for about 2 minutes. Remove and place on paper towels to drain. This is the first step of a two-step frying process and may be done up to 2 hours ahead of time. The first step cooks the potato and keeps it from turning brown. The second ensures a crispy texture.

8) At serving time, preheat oil to 325 degrees again. Fry the shrimp in small batches for 5 minutes, or until done. Place on new dry paper towels to absorb excess grease. Plate and serve with cocktail sauce.

SERVES 6

Pepper-Seared Beef Carpaccio

INGREDIENTS

3-4-pound beef tenderloin, center cut

½ cup finely-ground black pepper

4 tablespoons vegetable oil

1 cup Roasted Garlic Oil (recipe below)

Kosher salt

Fresh grated Parmesan

Arugula to garnish

Roasted Garlic Oil (recipe below)

METHOD

1) Cut the tenderloin lengthwise into 2 long semi-circles. Trim off a little of the corners to round off.

2) Pour pepper out onto a sheet tray. Roll the tenderloin in the ground black pepper. Let meat sit on the tray for 3-4 minutes and repeat.

3) Preheat a heavy-bottomed skillet or sauté pan on high heat.

4) When the pan is very hot, quickly pour in the vegetable oil to cover entire bottom of pan. Add 1 tenderloin piece at a time. Roll the tenderloin a little bit every few minutes until all outer surfaces have been seared. Remove the tenderloin, place it on a large plate and put it in the freezer.

5) Store the meat in the freezer until the meat is about 80 percent frozen. Remove from freezer and cut the meat into ⅛-inch-thick slices. Line a cutting board with plastic wrap. Place the slices on the plastic wrap close together but not touching. Cover all slices with another layer of plastic wrap. Use the flat side of a meat tenderizer mallet to flatten gently.

6) Return covered slices to freezer just long enough to freeze the meat enough to be picked up and arranged on a plate or serving tray. Remove plastic wrap carefully.

7) Place Roasted Garlic Oil in a small sauté pan over high heat. Warm the oil just until it is hot to the touch. Using a large spoon, liberally apply the hot oil over the slices of beef.

8) Season meat with kosher salt to taste.

9) Garnish with arugula, grilled bread and roasted garlic cloves.

SERVES 12

Roasted Garlic Oil

INGREDIENTS

2 cups peeled raw garlic cloves

2 cups olive oil

METHOD

1) Place garlic cloves and olive oil in a small pot over medium heat. Let come to a simmer and reduce heat to lowest setting. Cook until garlic is tender to the touch.

2) Remove from heat and let cool at room temperature. Refrigerate.

3) Strain garlic cloves from oil.

4) Reserve roasted garlic and oil from preparation of the Carpaccio, above.

It's Suppertime!

My mother would yell, "It's Suppertime!" and the slam of the old screen door quickly followed. After being reminded to wash our hands, my brother, sister and I would take our places at the table. Suppers at my parents' house included extended family–friends and farm hands–and they tended to linger. At Jonathan's, we call our entrées "suppers" with the same intention, that the meal be leisurely enjoyed with friends, family and co-workers. These are some of my favorite suppers.

Grilled rack of lamb with my Mint Julep Jelly. Mint and lamb are a classic combination. Bourbon and mint are also a classic Kentucky combination. My Mint Julep Jelly – in homage to the cocktail – brings the two together. First, I make a bourbon jelly, then fresh mint is blanched and puréed. The two components are mixed together just before being served. The unexpected freshness of the mint marries well with the succulence of the lamb. Pair this with my creamy, tangy Goat Cheese Scalloped Potatoes. The chewy bits around the edges are the best.

Red-eye gravy is a quick pan sauce made from country ham drippings and strong black coffee. It is typically served with buttermilk biscuits for breakfast. It is a favorite of mine and was the inspiration for my Coffee-Seared Pork Chops. Coffee beans, black peppercorns, cumin and coriander are toasted and ground in a spice mill. The chops are then coated in the spice mix, pan-seared and finished in the oven. I serve them with Sweet Corn Whipped Potatoes and a pool of Maker's Mark Red-Eye Gravy.

Kentuckians, like all Southerners, love barbeque. My grilled Barbequed Yellow Fin Tuna is a fresh, fast twist on the long-cooked, meat-centered tradition. A smoky tomato-based sauce with maple syrup for sweetness and coarsely-ground mustard to give it a bite is basted on the grilled fish. Crispy White Cheddar Grits and Maple-Mustard Slaw give this easy picnic supper great flair.

Kentucky-raised bison is braised with Kentucky Bourbon Barrel Ale until the sweet, rich meat is tender and the pan juices reduced into a wonderful sauce. This is the perfect dish for a cool fall evening. Serve it with my Fresh Horseradish Creamed Spinach and Mashed Potatoes.

Rainbow trout with a Crispy Black-Eyed Pea crust is my version of trout almondine. Black-eyed peas – soaked in water for 24 hours, drained, deep-fried and salted – are crushed to a breading consistency. The crusted fish is sautéed and served over Jasmine Rice. Its nutty, earthy, buttery crunch is magnified by a topping of Browned Butter, Wilted Limestone Bibb Lettuce and Caramelized Onions.

Though the influence was traditional Italian, my Country Ham Carbonara is pure Southern. Diced country ham is cooked in a skillet until it's rendered into crispy delicious bites. Soybeans, one of Kentucky's largest cash crops, stand in for the usual green peas. The sauce is made with Parmesan and egg yolks, as is the traditional sauce, but I do add a good amount of heavy cream before it's all tossed with Pappardelle pasta.

I could not resist sharing some other favorites. Of course, my interpretation of Shrimp and Grits and Skillet-Blackened Salmon are included, along with a few of my Southern-inspired signature dishes: Rock Salt-Roasted Chicken, Sorghum-Glazed Sea Scallops, Shiitake-Dusted Beef Tenderloin Medallions, and Duck Confit.

Remember, It's Suppertime!, so linger and enjoy.

IT'S SUPPERTIME!

Coffee-Seared Pork Chops

Maker's Mark Red-Eye Gravy

Black-Eyed Pea-
Crusted Trout

Skillet-Blackened Salmon

Barbequed Yellow Fin Tuna

Maple-Mustard Barbeque Sauce
Simple Tomato Barbeque Sauce

Country Ham Carbonara

Rock Salt-Roasted Chicken

Grilled Lamb Rack with
Mint Julep Jelly

Mint Julep Jelly

Shrimp and Grits

Sorghum-Glazed
Seared Sea Scallops

Buttermilk Whipped Cream

Cracker-Fried Oyster-
Stuffed Filet

Horseradish Gravy
Cracker-Fried Oysters

Kentucky Bourbon Barrel
Ale-Braised Bison Brisket

Shiitake-Dusted Beef
Tenderloin Medallions

Shiitake Dust
Caramel-Peppercorn Base
Caramel-Peppercorn Sauce

Duck Confit with Old
Fashioned Cherry Relish

Old Fashioned Cherry Relish
Old Fashioned Macerated Cherries

Coffee-Seared Pork Chops

Two techniques provide intense flavors for these signature pork chops. Toasting whole coffee beans and spices releases their natural oils. The mixture is ground to provide intense flavors and fragrances.

INGREDIENTS

6 center-cut pork chops

1 cup coffee beans

½ cup black peppercorns

1 tablespoon whole cumin seeds

3 tablespoons whole coriander

1 ½ tablespoons salt

1 tablespoon sugar

4 tablespoons vegetable oil

Maker's Mark Red-Eye Gravy (page 102)

METHOD

1) Preheat oven to 400 degrees Fahrenheit.

2) Place coffee beans, cumin and coriander on a cookie tray. Place in oven and bake for 2-3 minutes, just until the fragrance from the coffee and spices is released. Do not burn. Remove and allow mixture to cool.

3) Place in a coffee mill in small batches and pulse to produce a coarsely-ground mixture.

4) Mix ground coffee and spice mixture with salt and sugar. Set aside. Can be made ahead of time. Store in an airtight container until needed.

5) Lay the pork chops out and coat the top and bottom with the spice mixture.

6) Place the vegetable oil in a large skillet and preheat pan over medium heat. Sauté spice-rubbed pork chops for about 2 minutes on each side. Remove pork chops, then dump the oil out of the pan.

7) The pork chops can be held at room temperature for no more than an hour. Place in the a 400 degree farenheit oven right before serving. Bake the coffee-seared pork chops for about 4-5 minutes or until desired doneness. I suggest the pork be served medium to medium-well.

SERVES 6

Pairing notes: Coffee-Seared Pork Chops with Maker's Mark Red-Eye Gravy, Corn-Whipped Potatoes and Green Beans.

Maker's Mark Red-Eye Gravy

Red-eye gravy is a quick pan sauce made by cooking country ham steaks in a skillet and deglazing the pan with strong black coffee. In this adaptation of the traditional sauce, a few more ingredients are added, including Bourbon. Typically, red-eye gravy is served with buttermilk biscuits, grits and country ham as a traditional Southern breakfast.

INGREDIENTS

1 tablespoon vegetable oil

1½ pounds raw country ham scraps or steaks

1 cup sliced yellow onions

1 clove fresh garlic, crushed

1 small sprig fresh sage

2 cups strong brewed coffee

1 cup water

1 tablespoon Makers Mark Bourbon

METHOD

1) Simmer country ham steaks in vegetable oil in a large skillet over medium heat for about 5 minutes on each side.

2) Add the remainder of the ingredients except the Bourbon and continue to simmer for another 10 minutes.

3) Strain out the country ham scraps or steaks. If scraps were used to make the sauce, they can now be discarded.

4) Add Bourbon just prior to serving.

5) Sauce can be made ahead of time, stored in the refrigerator, and reheated at time of serving.

YIELDS 3 CUPS - SERVES 6

Pairing notes: *Coffee-Seared Pork Chops and Corn-Whipped Potatoes and Green Beans.*

Maker's Mark *is a trademarked product of the Maker's Mark Distillery, Inc., of Loretto, Kentucky.*

Black-Eyed Pea-Crusted Trout

Rainbow trout is a light-flavored, delicate freshwater fish, often crusted with nuts such as almonds. I like to crust trout using Crispy Black-Eyed Peas, acquainting the fish with my modern Southern cooking style.

INGREDIENTS

4 cups Crispy Black-Eyed Peas (page 27)

2 tablespoons yellow cornmeal

2 tablespoons flour

1 teaspoon freshly-ground black pepper

6 whole-boned trout fillets

4 eggs

2 cups milk

2 cups flour

METHOD

1) Place the Crispy Black-Eyed Peas, cornmeal, flour and pepper in a food processor. Purée the mixture to create a coarsely-ground breading. Place into a container large enough to dip the trout into.

2) Preheat oven to 350 degrees Fahrenheit.

3) Mix eggs and milk together in medium-sized bowl that is big enough to dip trout into.

4) Place the flour into a container large enough to hold the trout fillets.

5) Spray 2 sheet trays with pan release or brush them with melted butter. These trays will be used to bake the trout, and the oil or butter will prevent sticking.

6) Take each trout and dust the flesh side with flour.

7) Dip the flour-dusted trout into the egg wash on the flesh side.

8) Dip the trout into the black-eyed pea crust on the flesh side.

9) Place the crusted trout skin-side down on the sheet trays. Trout can be crusted a few hours before cooking and stored in a refrigerator.

10) Bake trout for about 7 minutes until cooked through.

SERVES 6

Pairing notes: *Black-Eyed Pea-Crusted Rainbow Trout with Jasmine Rice, Browned Butter and Wilted Limestone Bibb Lettuce. Garnish with Crispy Black-Eyed Peas.*

Cooking notes: *Trout can be breaded, placed on a sheet tray and held in the refrigerator until time of cooking.*

Skillet-Blackened Salmon

My Skillet-Blackened Salmon borrows from traditional Cajun cuisine and the modern adaptation of Chef Paul Prudhomme. Wild-caught salmon is dredged in butter, a mix of herbs and spices, then sautéed in a hot skillet. The spicy black charred crust complements the full-flavored fish perfectly.

INGREDIENTS

5 tablespoons paprika

¼ cup salt

4 tablespoons garlic powder

2 tablespoons freshly-ground black pepper

2 tablespoons onion powder

3 tablespoons cayenne powder

2 tablespoons dried oregano

2 tablespoons dried thyme

½ pound melted butter

6 (7-8-ounce) skinless/boneless salmon filets

METHOD

1) Mix all herbs and spices together thoroughly.

2) Place a large cast iron skillet on high heat and allow it to become very hot.

3) Turn on stovetop vent if available, as this cooking process will produce lots of smoke and will likely set off your kitchen smoke detector.

4) Dip the salmon filets into the butter, then into the spice mixture and place in the hot skillet.

5) Sear the fish for about 2 minutes on each side. Remove and place on sheet tray. This step can be done about 30-45 minutes prior to serving and finished in a 400 degree Fahrenheit oven for about 5-7 minutes, or until desired doneness.

SERVES 6

Pairing notes: *Skillet-Blackened Salmon, Crawfish Corn Pudding and Soybean Succotash.*

Cooking notes: *I prefer salmon to be served medium well.*

Barbequed Yellow Fin Tuna

INGREDIENTS

8 (6-8 ounce) portions
yellow fin tuna

2 tablespoons salt

1 tablespoon freshly-
ground black pepper

2-3 tablespoons vegetable
oil to brush grill before
grilling tuna

7 cups Maple-Mustard
Barbeque Sauce (page 110)

6 portions Crispy
White Cheddar Grits
(page 179)

3 cups Maple Mustard
Slaw (page 184)

METHOD

1) Follow Maple-Mustard Slaw recipe. Store in refrigerator until last-minute plating.

2) Follow Crispy White Cheddar Grits recipe and have them pre-fried and holding in a 200 degree Fahrenheit oven.

3) Preheat grill. If using charcoal, allow the flames to burn down to the point when you can hold your hand over the flames for at least 5 seconds. If you are unable to do so, the fire is too hot. Let the fire burn down a little until not so hot. If using a gas grill, adjust the flames to appropriate cooking temperature after the preheating process.

4) Rub grill down with vegetable oil.

5) Season tuna with desired amounts of salt and pepper.

6) Place the tuna steaks on a grill and grill them for about 2-3 minutes, then turn each 90 degrees for another 2-3 minutes to develop good square grill marks. Flip tuna steaks over and repeat process. While tuna is cooking, baste the fish with the Maple Mustard Barbeque Sauce.

7) Remove tuna from grill just a little underdone, slightly under the desired temperature. It will keep cooking.

8) Plate the tuna with the grits, slaw and more warmed barbeque sauce.

SERVES 8

Pairing notes: *Barbequed Tuna, Crispy White Cheddar Grits, Maple-Mustard Slaw*

Cooking notes: *I prefer tuna to be served medium rare.*

Maple-Mustard Barbeque Sauce

INGREDIENTS

6 cups Simple Tomato
Barbeque Sauce (page 111)

½ cup whole ground
mustard

1 cup maple syrup

METHOD

1) Mix all ingredients together. Simmer on low heat until hot.

2) Can be made up to 1 week ahead of time. Store in a refrigerator. Reheat before serving.

YIELDS ABOUT 7 CUPS

Simple Tomato Barbeque Sauce

INGREDIENTS

8 cups good quality whole canned tomatoes

2 tablespoons vegetable oil

2 yellow onions, finely-diced

2 tablespoons chopped garlic

1 tablespoon dried thyme

12-ounce bottle Kentucky Bourbon Barrel Ale or other light beer.

4 cups tomato juice, reserved from canned tomatoes

1¼ cups brown sugar

1 cup cider vinegar

2 teaspoons chipotle chilies in adobo sauce

½ tablespoon cold water

½ tablespoon cornstarch

METHOD

1) Open canned tomatoes and strain through a colander over a large bowl. While tomatoes are draining, slice the tomatoes in half and press out excess liquid. Reserve liquid for later use.

2) Smoke the tomatoes in a home smoker for about 15 minutes, following manufacturer's instructions. If you do not have a home smoker, this step could be skipped.

3) In a large pot, preheat the vegetable oil and sauté the onions, garlic and thyme for 2-3 minutes. De-glaze the pan with the Kentucky Ale. Simmer beer for 3-4 minutes to cook off alcohol from the pot. Add remaining ingredients except water and cornstarch.

4) Heat the cornstarch and water in a separate container. Pour into barbeque sauce and stir to incorporate. Simmer an additional 2 minutes. Allow mixture to simmer on medium heat for about 30 minutes or until reduced by half. Remove from heat and cool at room temperature.

5) Place the cooled sauce into a blender and purée until smooth.

6) Place the puréed sauce into a clean pot and bring back to a simmer on medium heat. Mix the cool water and cornstarch together. Stir cornstarch mixture into sauce and continue to simmer for about 5 minutes, stirring often to keep the sauce from sticking to the bottom of the pan and burning. As the sauce reduces, scrape down the sides of the pan with a heatproof rubber spatula.

7) Remove from heat and allow to cool. Store sauce in a refrigerator until needed. Can be made up to 1 week ahead of time.

YIELDS 6 CUPS

Country Ham Carbonara

INGREDIENTS

10 ounces raw country ham, trimmed and cubed

3 tablespoon olive oil

½ small-diced yellow onion

2 cloves garlic, minced

1 cup white wine

1½ cups Chicken Stock (page 59)

2½ cups heavy cream

2 egg yolks

1 pound cooked Pappardelle pasta

1 ½ cups shredded Parmesan cheese

1 cup soybeans, cooked and shelled, or substitute peas or lima beans

1 ½ cups halved cherry tomatoes

1 teaspoon salt

½ teaspoon freshly-ground black pepper

METHOD

1) Add country ham and 1 tablespoon olive oil to a medium-sized sauté pan. Cook over medium heat for 10-12 minutes or until ham is slightly crispy. Remove from pan and drain on paper towel.

2) Preheat the oil used to cook the ham in a large sauté pan over high heat. Add diced onions and sauté for about 2-3 minutes. Add garlic and sauté for another 1-2 minutes. De-glaze pan with white wine. Continue to cook for another 3-4 minutes or until alcohol has cooked off.

3) Add Chicken Stock and cream. Reduce heat to a simmer. Whisk in egg yolks. Continue to simmer until sauce slightly thickens, about 2-3 minutes.

4) Add pasta. Simmer for another 2-3 minutes.

5) Sprinkle Parmesan cheese over pasta. Stir to incorporate.

6) Add soybeans, cherry tomatoes, salt and pepper.

SERVES 4-6

Rock Salt-Roasted Chicken

This simple chicken dish is delicious and easy to prepare. It can also be partially pre-cooked for easy production for entertaining. This main course has consistently been on the menu at my restaurant for a decade and has been requested more than any other.

INGREDIENTS

12 small to medium-sized bone-in, skin-on chicken breasts

½ cup rock salt (kosher salt can be substituted)

2 cups flour

¾ cup vegetable oil

METHOD

1) Preheat oven to 400 degrees Fahrenheit.

2) Crush rock salt in a coffee mill. Pulse the machine until coarse grinding is achieved. Crushed salt should be slightly larger than kosher salt crystals. If using kosher salt, no need to grind.

3) Lay chicken breasts out on a tray and sprinkle each with about 2 teaspoons salt on the skin side only.

4) Dredge the chicken breast, skin side only, in flour.

5) Preheat large sauté pan with the vegetable oil.

6) Sear chicken breasts a few at a time, skin side first, to develop a light tan crust. This should only take a few minutes. Flip chicken and cook for 2 minutes on other side. Remove from pan and place on a sheet pan, skin side up.

7) The chicken is then placed in the oven to cook thoroughly. The chicken can also be set aside for an hour or so and then finished in the oven. Chicken will take about 8-10 minutes, depending on chicken breast size.

SERVES 6

Pairing notes: *Rock Salt-Roasted Chicken with Roasted Garlic Mashed Potatoes and Butter-Poached Asparagus*

Cooking notes: *I do not suggest skinless chicken breasts for this dish. Bone-in chicken breasts produce a better dish, but you can use boneless breasts. Large breasts will need to be roasted longer, in a slightly cooler oven, for proper cooking.*

Grilled Lamb Rack with Mint Julep Jelly

INGREDIENTS

3 frenched lamb racks, typically 7-8 chops per rack

Salt and pepper to taste

1 cup Mint Julep Jelly (page 118)

METHOD

1) Lamb racks can be purchased from most butchers. The term "frenched" refers to the meat and fat that are trimmed out to expose the bone, done primarily for aesthetic reasons.

2) If you buy lamb that has not been frenched and plan to do this yourself, make sure you ask if the chine bone has been removed.

3) Cut chops out of the racks by slicing the meat between the bones. Lay out on a tray, and season with salt and pepper.

4) Grill lamb chops for about 5-6 minutes each side.

5) Serve with Mint Julep Jelly

SERVES 6-8

Pairing notes: Grilled Lamb Rack Chops with Mint Julep Jelly and Goat Cheese Scalloped Potatoes.

Cooking notes: It is possible to mark your lamb on the grill a few hours before serving and to place it on a baking sheet to finish cooking it at 400 degrees Fahrenheit before serving. Lamb rack chops are a fatty cut of meat. The grill is likely to flame up from the dripping fat during the grilling. Have a small container of water available to help put out flame-ups, which will also impart a burned flavor to the lamb.

Mint Julep Jelly

English culinary tradition often pairs roasted lamb with mint jelly. Commercially-made, green-colored mint jelly is widely available in most supermarkets. My version of the classic combination embraces the Bluegrass through the use of Bourbon and fresh mint.

INGREDIENTS

2 cups good quality Bourbon

2 cups water

1 package (1.75 oz) fruit pectin

5 cups sugar

1 teaspoon salt

½ teaspoon freshly-ground black pepper

2 cups packed fresh mint leaves

2 cups water

METHOD

1) Place the Bourbon and 2 cups water in a four-quart pot and bring to a boil.

2) Stir in the fruit pectin. Bring back to a boil.

3) Stir in the sugar, salt and pepper. Bring back to a full rolling boil.

4) Reduce the heat and simmer for 10 minutes. Remove from heat and pour into a heat-proof container for storage.

5) It is best to make the Bourbon jelly base at least 24 hours in advance and to store it in the refrigerator to allow the jelly to set fully. It may be stored in a refrigerator for up to 2 weeks.

6) A few hours before service, pick mint leaves from the stem. You will need approximately ½ pound to yield the 2 packed cups of mint leaves for the jelly.

7) In a small pot, bring the second 2 cups of water to a full boil. When water is boiling, drop the mint into the water and stir for about 30 seconds. Quickly dump the mint and water into a strainer, discarding the liquid. The mint is then submerged into ice-cold water. When the mint is cooled, strain again. Using your hand, squeeze all excess liquid from the mint.

8) A few moments before serving, place the blanched mint in a blender with 1 cup of the Bourbon jelly and purée until smooth. Mix with 2 more cups of Bourbon jelly.

YIELDS ABOUT 8 CUPS

Cooking notes: *The Bourbon jelly base may be made in advance, but the mint purée should only be mixed in at the very last minute.*

Shrimp and Grits

There are many variations on Shrimp and Grits. Sometimes the dish is made with bacon, sometimes with sausage. Other variations involve sauces. Some are tomato-based and others are simply sautéed with butter, lemon and parsley. My version uses a slightly spicy, tomato-based sauce in which the shrimp is simmered, then finished with butter.

Another unique characteristic of this recipe involves the preparation of the grits. The grits are cooked with water, cream and cheese, then they are poured out and allowed to cool and set up firm. Afterward, the grits are cut and pan-fried to develop a wonderful blend of crispness outside and creaminess inside.

INGREDIENTS

1 tablespoon vegetable oil

½ cup diced yellow onion

½ cup diced celery

½ cup diced green bell pepper

½ jalapeno pepper, seeds removed

2 cloves garlic, minced

1 tablespoon fresh basil, chopped

1 tablespoon fresh thyme

2 bay leaves

1 cup canned tomatoes

1 cup tomato juice

1 cup Shrimp or Chicken Stock (pages 59, 60) or vegetable stock

½ teaspoon salt

¼ teaspoon cayenne pepper

½ tablespoon freshly-ground black pepper

2 pounds large peeled and deveined shrimp

4 tablespoons cold butter

Crispy White Cheddar Grits (page 179)

METHOD

1) In a 4-quart pot, preheat the vegetable oil and sauté the onions, celery and green bell peppers on high heat until tender. Add garlic, jalapeno pepper and herbs, and continue to sauté for 2 more minutes.

2) Add the remainder of the ingredients except the shrimp and lower heat to simmer for 20 minutes.

3) Remove the sauce from the heat and allow it to cool. Place in a blender and purée to a smooth consistency. This can be done as much as a few days ahead of time and stored in the refrigerator.

4) Place the shrimp and the refrigerated sauce into a large pot. Place the pot over low heat, stirring every few minutes to ensure even cooking. The shrimp will need to be simmered for about 10 minutes. Just before the shrimp is done cooking, stir in the butter.

5) Quickly pick out the shrimp and set aside. On each plate, ladle about 3-4 ounces of sauce.

6) Place Crispy White Cheddar Grits over the sauce and then stand the shrimp up in the grits.

SERVES 6-8

Pairing Notes: *Crispy White Cheddar Grits.*

Cooking notes: *Overcooking the shrimp will greatly reduce the quality of this dish. Both the grits and sauce can be prepped early, leaving only the shrimp to be cooked and plated, making this an easy dish for entertaining.*

121

Sorghum-Glazed Seared Sea Scallops

INGREDIENTS

16 large dry-packed fresh
sea scallops

1 tablespoon olive oil

3 tablespoons
chilled butter

1 teaspoon salt

½ teaspoon freshly-ground
black pepper

1 cup sorghum

Cornbread Skillet Cakes
(page 183)

Bacon-Wilted Baby Spinach
(page 188)

Buttermilk Whipped Cream
(page 56)

METHOD

1) Preheat oven to 450 degrees Fahrenheit.

2) Place scallops on paper towels to absorb excess moisture.

2) Preheat a thick-bottomed sauté pan or skillet on high heat.

3) Add olive oil and then sea scallops. Sear scallops for 2-3 minutes on one side only. Do not flip scallops over.

4) Add the chilled butter to the pan and transfer to oven. Bake for about 4-5 minutes. Remove when scallops are still just slightly undercooked.

5) Remove from the pan and let the scallops rest on a paper towel bed. Season the scallops with salt and pepper. Place 4 scallops, seared side up, onto each plate with Cornbread Skillet Cakes, Bacon Wilted Spinach and Buttermilk Whipped Cream. Ladle 1 tablespoon of sorghum on each scallop.

SERVES 4

Cracker-Fried Oyster-Stuffed Filet

INGREDIENTS

6 8-ounce beef
tenderloin filets

12 Cracker-Fried Oysters
(page 127)

2 tablespoons salt

1 tablespoon freshly-
ground black pepper

Mashed Potatoes
(page 192)

Fresh Horseradish-Creamed
Spinach (page 189)

Horseradish Gravy
(page 126)

METHOD

1) Preheat oven to 400 degrees Fahrenheit.

2) Preheat grill. Rub grill with oil to prevent steaks from sticking. Grill steaks for about 3-4 minutes on each side. Remove from grill and place on sheet tray. This step can be done up to an hour before serving.

3) Follow Cracker-Fried Oysters recipe. When almost ready to fry oysters, place meat in oven to finish cooking. Cooking time should be about 8-10 minutes for medium temperature.

4) When steaks are at desired temperature, cut a small pocket in the side of each filet and stuff with a Cracker-Fried Oyster.

5) Garnish each of the filets with another Cracker-Fried Oyster.

6) Serve the filets with Mashed Potatoes, Fresh Horseradish-Creamed Spinach and Horseradish Gravy.

SERVES 6

Horseradish Gravy

INGREDIENTS

4 tablespoons butter, melted

4 tablespoons flour

2 cups Brown Beef Stock (page 61) or broth

3 tablespoons prepared horseradish, with moisture squeezed out

1 tablespoon whole-grain mustard

½ teaspoon salt

¼ teaspoon freshly-ground black pepper

METHOD

1) To make roux, mix butter and flour in a small sauté pan. Place on low heat and stir often. Cook roux for about 5 minutes. Remove from heat and set aside.

2) Place Brown Beef Stock in a small saucepan and bring to a boil.

3) Place roux in a small bowl and ladle about ½ cup of hot stock into bowl. Whisk mixture until it becomes thick and smooth. Ladle in another ½ cup of hot stock and repeat. Pour mixture into hot stock and whisk until smooth. Simmer on low heat for 5 minutes.

4) Season thickened stock, horseradish, whole-grain mustard, salt and black pepper.

5) Serve hot, or refrigerate for up to 3 days. Reheat over low heat.

YIELDS 2¼ CUPS · SERVES 6

Cracker-Fried Oysters

INGREDIENTS

12 shucked oysters

1 teaspoon salt

½ teaspoon freshly-ground black pepper

6 eggs

2 cups milk

2 cups flour

1 pound hand-crushed saltine crackers

1 cup vegetable oil

METHOD

1) Drain oysters in a colander. Season oysters with salt and pepper.

2) To make egg wash, crack eggs into a medium-sized bowl. Add milk and whisk until fully incorporated.

3) Place flour in a medium-sized bowl.

4) Place crushed crackers in a medium-sized bowl.

5) Place oysters, one at a time, into the flour, making sure oysters are coated well. Shake off excess flour and drop into egg wash.

6) Using a pair of tongs, grab one oyster at a time and place into the crushed crackers. Toss oyster around in the bowl and press down slightly with hands to flatten. Remove and place on a wax paper-lined sheet tray. Repeat process till all oysters have been cracker-breaded.

7) Preheat oven to 250 degrees Fahrenheit.

8) Preheat oil to 350 degrees Fahrenheit in large sauté pan. Place about half of the oysters in hot oil and sauté for about 2-3 minutes each side. Remove from pan and place on a paper towel-lined sheet tray. Store oysters on a sheet pan in the oven while second half of oysters are being cooked.

SERVES 6

Kentucky Bourbon Barrel Ale-Braised Bison Brisket

Bison brisket is similar to beef brisket, but is much leaner and has more flavor. Braising the meat with Kentucky Bourbon Barrel Ale adds a pleasant sweetness.

INGREDIENTS FOR BRAISING

6-8 pounds bison brisket, or beef brisket

2 tablespoons vegetable oil

5 cloves peeled fresh garlic

4 cups chopped celery

4 cups chopped yellow onions

4 cups chopped peeled carrots

2 bay leaves

1 tablespoon whole black peppercorns

1-inch sprig fresh rosemary

10 sprigs fresh thyme

6 12-ounce bottles Kentucky Bourbon Barrel Ale

INGREDIENTS FOR SAUCE

½ gallon braising liquids from cooking the brisket

2 12-ounce bottles Kentucky Bourbon Barrel Ale

2 tablespoons salt

1 teaspoon freshly-ground pepper

1 tablespoon sugar

2 tablespoons cornstarch

2 tablespoons cool water

METHOD

1) Preheat oven to 350 degrees Fahrenheit.

2) Preheat large skillet with vegetable oil. Sear bison brisket for 5-6 minutes on each side. Remove brisket from pan and set into a large, 4-inch-deep roasting pan.

3) Use the same skillet to sauté garlic, celery, onions and carrots for about 5 minutes to develop noticeable caramelization on the vegetables. Dump vegetables into the roasting pan.

4) Add remaining ingredients to the roasting pan.

5) Cover roasting pan with aluminum foil.

6) Roast for about 3 hours. Remove from oven and check meat for tenderness. Bison should be tender to the touch. If not done, return to oven and cook for another 20-30 minutes.

7) When tender, allow bison to cool to room temperature. Remove from braising liquids and refrigerate.

8) When thoroughly cooled, cut bison into 6-8-ounce portions (about ½-inch thick).

9) Save scraps in an airtight container in the refrigerator for other uses, like burgoo.

10) Store portioned bison in an airtight container in the refrigerator.

11) Strain braising liquids through a fine-mesh strainer. Discard vegetables and herbs. Save liquids.

12) Place reserved braising liquid in a medium-sized pot and add 2 bottles Kentucky Bourbon Barrel Ale, salt, pepper and sugar. Bring to a boil.

13) When mixture comes to a boil, mix cornstarch and 2 tablespoons cool water in a small bowl and then stir into pot. Simmer for 10 minutes.

14) At time of serving, place the portioned bison brisket in a baking dish with enough of the sauce to half-cover the meat. Cover with foil and bake in a 400 degree Fahrenheit oven for about 10 minutes. Remove bison and place on plate. Ladle a little more sauce over the meat and serve.

SERVES 6-8

Pairing notes: Kentucky Bourbon Barrel Ale-Braised Bison Brisket with Fresh Horseradish Creamed Spinach.

Cooking notes: Cook brisket a day or two ahead of time and reheat, covered, in a 350-degree Fahrenheit oven.

Shiitake-Dusted Beef Tenderloin Medallions

INGREDIENTS

12 3-4-ounce beef tenderloin medallions

Shiitake Dust (page 132), as needed

4-6 ounces vegetable oil

1 cup Crispy Shiitake "Bacon" (page 157)

Caramel-Peppercorn Sauce (page 133)

METHOD

1) Preheat oven to 400 degrees Fahrenheit.

2) Place the beef medallions on a sheet tray lined with Shiitake Dust. Place more Shiitake Dust over the top of each medallion. Press down on the tenderloin with your hands to thoroughly coat the medallions. Squeeze the sides of the tenderloins to return them back to their original shape. Flip tenderloins over and repeat process.

3) Preheat a large sauté pan with the vegetable oil. Sear the medallions for about 2-3 minutes each side. Remove the medallions from the pan and place on a sheet tray. Medallions can be pre-seared and kept at room temperature until ready to cook at the very last minute.

4) Cook to desired temperature in oven.

5) Ladle Caramel-Peppercorn Sauce over each serving, then garnish with Crispy Shiitake "Bacon."

SERVES 6

Shiitake Dust

INGREDIENTS

4-5 cups dried
shiitake mushrooms

1 teaspoon dried thyme

1 ½ tablespoons salt

2 teaspoons freshly-ground
black pepper

2 teaspoons garlic powder

2 teaspoons onion powder

METHOD

1) Place dried mushrooms in a food processor and purée until a coarsely-ground powder is achieved. Measure out 1 cup.

2) Mix the cup of mushroom powder with the remaining ingredients.

3) Set aside until needed. Can be made ahead of time and stored at room temperature in an airtight container.

YIELDS 1 ½ CUPS

Caramel-Peppercorn Sauce

INGREDIENTS

4 tablespoons butter, melted

4 tablespoons flour

3 cups Brown Beef Stock (page 61)

½ cup Caramel Peppercorn Base (recipe below)

METHOD

1) To make roux, mix butter and flour in a small sauté pan. Place on low heat and stir often. Cook roux for about 5 minutes. Remove from heat and set aside.

2) Place Brown Beef Stock in small saucepan and bring to a boil.

3) Place roux in a small bowl and ladle about ½ cup of hot stock into bowl. Whisk mixture until it becomes thick and smooth. Ladle in another ½ cup of hot stock and repeat. Pour mixture into hot stock and whisk until smooth. Simmer on low heat for 5 minutes.

4) Season thickened stock with ½ cup of Caramel Peppercorn Base.

5) Serve hot, or refrigerate for up to 3 days. Reheat over low heat.

YIELDS ABOUT 4 CUPS

Caramel-Peppercorn Base

INGREDIENTS

1 pound beef scraps from the chain of a whole tenderloin, roughly-chopped

3 tablespoons kosher salt

4 tablespoons cracked black peppercorns

1¼ pounds brown sugar

METHOD

1) Purchase a whole beef tenderloin. When cleaning and portioning the tenderloin you will have scraps that you can utilize as a base flavor for the Caramel Peppercorn Sauce. Weigh out 1 to 1½ pounds of scrap meat from the chain, a long strip from the side of the tenderloin not served.

2) In a mixing bowl, blend the brown sugar, salt and crushed peppercorns.

3) Place the meat, surrounded by the sugar and spice mixture, in a storage container with a tight-fitting lid and store in a refrigerator for 48 hours. The mixture will draw out flavors and moisture from the meat and turn into a coarse meal syrup.

4) Place the sugar and meat mixture into a small pot over medium heat and melt the mixture to syrup.

5) Remove the meat scraps and discard. Store syrup in a refrigerator until needed for up to a week.

YIELDS 1 CUP

133

Duck Confit with Old Fashioned Cherry Relish

INGREDIENTS

¾ cup kosher salt

½ teaspoon ground cinnamon

¼ teaspoon ground nutmeg

¼ teaspoon ground allspice

12 duck hindquarters, leg and thigh attached

10 cups rendered duck fat, lard or olive oil, or combination of these

12 cloves garlic, smashed

4 tablespoons whole black peppercorns

12 bay leaves

16-20 sprigs fresh thyme

METHOD

1) Mix salt, cinnamon, nutmeg and allspice in a small bowl.

2) Lay duck out on a wire rack over a sheet tray. Sprinkle about 1 tablespoon of spice mixture over duck. Place in a refrigerator to dry, uncovered, for 24 hours.

3) Place dried salted duck legs into 2 separate, tall, 6 x 9 baking dishes. Cover the duck with the duck fat, lard or olive oil. Add bay leaves and thyme. Cover dish with plastic wrap and then with aluminum foil.

4) Preheat oven to 140 degrees Fahrenheit.

5) Place the fat-covered duck leg into the oven and bake it for 8-10 hours. It sounds complicated, but this slow cooking method is very easy. Just place it into the oven and go to sleep. Wake up in the morning, remove from the oven and unwrap. If your oven will not hold a low temperature of 140, then bake at 250 degrees Fahrenheit for about 4-6 hours, or until very tender.

6) Allow duck to cool at room temperature. When cool, remove duck from the fat and then refrigerate. This step can be done up to 3 days ahead of time.

7) To reheat duck, place in a 400-degree Fahrenheit oven for about 10-12 minutes and serve.

SERVES 6

Pairing notes: *Foie Gras Bread Pudding, Green Beans and Old Fashioned Cherry Relish.*

Old Fashioned Cherry Relish

INGREDIENTS

1 teaspoon vegetable oil

1 medium-sized red onion, small-diced

2 cups Bourbon

½ cup Grand Marnier

1 cup orange juice, fresh

2 tablespoons bitters

4 cups sugar

6 cups Old Fashioned Macerated Cherries (page 137)

3 cups fresh orange segments

METHOD

1) Sauté the red onion with the vegetable oil in a sauté pan for 2-3 minutes, or until tender. Remove from heat and add Bourbon and Grand Marnier. Carefully return to the heat, expecting a flame-up from the alcohol.

2) Add the orange juice, bitters and sugar. Simmer the mixture until reduced by half. Remove from heat and cool.

3) Add macerated cherries and orange segments.

4) Serve at room temperature.

YIELDS 6 CUPS

Old Fashioned Macerated Cherries

INGREDIENTS

2 pounds fresh cherries, washed and pitted (about 5 cups)

2 cups sugar

½ cup Grand Marnier

2 tablespoons honey

2 tablespoons Bourbon

METHOD

1) Place sugar, Bourbon, Grand Marnier and honey in a medium-sized pot. Place on stovetop and bring to a boil on high heat.

2) Reduce heat and simmer for five minutes.

3) Add pitted cherries.

4) Simmer for 5 minutes more.

5) Remove from heat. Allow cherries to cool at room temperature.

6) Store in a refrigerator for up to 2 weeks.

YIELDS 6 CUPS

Pairing notes: *Jonathan's Old Fashioned*

Cooking notes: *Only use fresh cherries.*

Bluegrass Brunches

With its in-between hour and characteristically gentler pace, brunch surely must have been born in the South. The traditional dishes of this leisurely practice tend to be uncomplicated and soul warming. Sauces coddle everything from Browns to Benedicts. Oddly, for all their casual intent and appearance, it is here that the quality of the ingredients and attention to detail make the most difference.

Eggs Benedict is ubiquitous. The most important component in the dish — and often its biggest flaw — is the sauce. Hollandaise is not complicated to make. It's just a matter of following precise but simple steps. I will teach you how to be flawless, first, and then you can be versatile. My Southern Eggs Benedict is made with Fried Green Tomatoes and country ham.

At the restaurant, we wanted to create a moist, crisp waffle that wouldn't become soggy. It was a quest with a happy result. I added cornmeal to the dry ingredients and folded fresh whipped egg whites into the wet ingredients. These waffles can stand up to any sauce.

I defy the Southern practice of using canned salmon when making salmon croquettes. This is the best example of how an inferior ingredient can ruin a great dish. I only use fresh salmon. My salmon cakes are sautéed and topped with a vine-ripened Tomato Dill Relish, asparagus and a freshly-made dill Hollandaise Sauce.

The Hot Brown was originally created at the Brown Hotel in Louisville, Kentucky. It is a simple, hot, open-faced sandwich, the success of which is, again, wholly dependent upon the quality of the ingredients used in its preparation. I use fresh roasted turkey breast, Colonel Bill Newsom's Aged Kentucky Country Ham, vine-ripened tomatoes and Applewood Smoked Bacon, all layered over thick-sliced bread and finished in a white cheddar cream sauce. It is first baked, then broiled until the top starts to brown. Make these in individual baking dishes if you can — they make serving easy and pretty.

My Crispy Shiitake "Bacon" Omelet, topped with shiitake mushroom "bacon" is the restaurant's most popular vegetarian brunch item. Slicing the locally grown mushrooms very thin and frying them at a low temperature transforms them into a crispy textured sensation.

BLUEGRASS BRUNCHES

Southern Eggs Benedict

Cornmeal Waffles with Bananas Foster Sauce and Toasted Pecans
Bananas Foster Sauce

Fresh Salmon Croquettes
Tomato Dill Relish
Hollandaise Sauce

Hot Brown
Hot Brown Sauce

Breakfast Home Fries

Ruby Red Grapefruit Brûlée

Crispy Shiitake "Bacon" Omelet
Crispy Shiitake "Bacon"

Southern Eggs Benedict

INGREDIENTS

1 gallon water

2 cups cider vinegar

14 large eggs

6 English muffins,
cut into halves

1½ pounds thin-sliced
cooked country ham

12 Fried Green Tomato
slices (page 17)

2 cups Hollandaise Sauce
(page 149)

METHOD

1) Place water and vinegar into a medium-sized pot. Place pot on stovetop and bring to a boil over high heat. Reduce heat to about 210 degrees Fahrenheit. The water should be just below a boil.

2) Carefully crack open eggs into the water. Cook for about 3-4 minutes. Remove with slotted spoon and place on a plate.

3) Stack the ham on the toasted English muffins. Next, lay Fried Green Tomatoes over ham, and cooked egg over each Fried Green Tomato.

4) Top each egg with about 2 ounces of Hollandaise Sauce.

SERVES 6

Cooking notes: *You will only need 12 eggs for this recipe, but it is a good idea to make extras. Sometimes the yolks will break during the plating process. Having extras on hand will also allow you to check doneness of eggs before you remove them all from the heat. Some people prefer their yolks runny, while others like the eggs to be fully cooked. In all cases, the whites of the eggs should be fully cooked.*

Cornmeal Waffles with Bananas Foster Sauce and Toasted Pecans

The cornmeal waffle batter presented in this recipe produces a light airy waffle, which maintains a crisp texture even after drizzling with maple syrup. Top these waffles off with toasted pecans and sliced bananas, or feel free to be creative.

INGREDIENTS

½ cup flour

½ cup cornstarch

½ cup cornmeal

1 tablespoon salt

1 teaspoon baking powder

½ teaspoon baking soda

2 tablespoons sugar

1 teaspoon vanilla extract

1½ cups buttermilk

½ cup milk

¾ cup vegetable oil

1 egg yolks

3 egg whites

Bananas Foster Sauce (page 145)

½ cup toasted pecans

METHOD

1) Sift all dry ingredients into a large mixing bowl.
2) In another large mixing bowl, mix the vanilla, buttermilk, milk, vegetable oil and egg yolks together.
3) Whip egg whites to a soft peak.
4) Mix all ingredients together.
5) Store in a refrigerator. May be made up to 2 hours before cooking.
6) Follow waffle machine directions.
7) Top off waffles with Bananas Foster Sauce and toasted pecans.

SERVES 6

Pairing notes: *Cornmeal Waffles with sliced bananas and sweet onion sausage.*

Cooking notes: *Keep batter in refrigerator or on ice. Batter works best when chilled.*

Bananas Foster Sauce

INGREDIENTS

1 stick butter, melted

2 cups brown sugar

½ teaspoon ground cinnamon

½ cup banana liqueur

6 bananas,
sliced ½-inch thick

½ cup dark rum

METHOD

1) Add melted butter, brown sugar and cinnamon in a medium-sized sauté pan. Place pan on low heat and simmer until sugar has dissolved.

2) Add remaining ingredients and simmer for 5 minutes.

3) Ladle 3-4 ounces on each portion of cornmeal waffles.

YIELDS ABOUT 4 CUPS - SERVES 6

Fresh Salmon Croquettes

INGREDIENTS

1 ½ pounds fresh salmon, cut into ¼-inch cubes

½ cup grated yellow onions

1 cup brioche breadcrumbs

¼ cup mayonnaise

4 tablespoons small-diced red bell peppers

4 tablespoons small-diced yellow bell peppers

½ teaspoon salt

¼ teaspoon ground white pepper

2 cups brioche breadcrumbs, for dusting before sautéeing.

½ cup vegetable oil

METHOD

1) Mix all ingredients except vegetable oil and 2 cups of the brioche breadcrumbs reserved for dusting the croquettes.

2) Divide mixture into 12 equal portions.

3) Form into cakes.

4) Coat cakes in remaining brioche breadcrumbs.

5) Place oil in a large sauté pan and preheat on medium heat.

6) Sauté cakes for about 3 minutes on each side or until golden brown crust is developed and the cakes are cooked throughout.

7) Remove from pan and serve.

S E R V E S   6

Pairing notes: *Fresh Salmon Croquettes with vine-ripened Tomato Dill Relish and Hollandaise Sauce.*

Cooking notes: *Brioche breadcrumbs can be replaced with other breadcrumbs.*

Tomato Dill Relish

INGREDIENTS

1 ½ cups vine-ripened
tomatoes, diced into
1 centimeter cubes

2 tablespoons finely-diced
red onions

2 tablespoons chopped
fresh dill

1 teaspoon sherry vinegar

1 tablespoon extra virgin
olive oil

½ teaspoon salt

¼ teaspoon freshly-ground
black pepper

½ teaspoon sugar

METHOD

1) Mix all ingredients.
2) Can be made up to a day ahead of time.

SERVES 6

148

Hollandaise Sauce

INGREDIENTS

4 egg yolks

1½ cups melted butter

1 tablespoon freshly-squeezed lemon juice

2 dashes Tabasco sauce

2 dashes Worcestershire sauce

1 pinch salt

Pairing notes: Southern Eggs Benedict and Fresh Salmon Croquettes.

Cooking Notes: *May add fresh dill for pairing with Fresh Salmon Croquettes.*

METHOD

1) Crack open eggs and carefully separate yolks from whites. Place yolks in small stainless steel bowl and whip for about 1 minute with a wire whisk.

2) Stir in lemon juice.

3) Place bowl over, but not in contact with, simmering water. Stir continuously while the bowl is over simmering water. In 3-5 minutes, the yolks will start to thicken slightly. Remove from heat.

4) If you notice the egg cooking around the edges, it means you have started to scramble the eggs and it will be necessary to start over.

5) Slowly pour melted butter into the bowl while stirring.

6) Season with Tabasco sauce, Worcestershire sauce and salt.

7) Can be made up to 1 hour prior to serving.

8) Store, covered, at room temperature, until needed.

YIELDS 2 CUPS

Hot Brown

A Hot Brown is a hot, open-faced sandwich originally created at the Brown Hotel in Louisville, Kentucky, in the early 1900s. Hot Browns appear on many Kentucky restaurant menus but, of course, I have created what I consider to be the best one ever. I use fresh roasted turkey breast, Colonial Bill Newsom's Aged Kentucky Country Ham, tomatoes and Applewood Smoked Bacon over thick-sliced bread and I finish it with a white cheddar cream sauce. The dish is baked, then broiled, just until the top starts to brown. It is served in its own baking dish.

INGREDIENTS

12 slices brioche bread (feel free to substitute any sandwich bread)

1 pound thinly-sliced cooked country ham

1 pound thinly-sliced roast turkey (avoid processed turkey loaf)

5 cups Hot Brown Sauce (recipe below)

6 ¼-inch tomato slices

12 slices cooked bacon

METHOD

1) Preheat oven to 450 degrees Fahrenheit.
2) Toast bread in a toaster until lightly colored and crispy.
3) In individual baking dishes (suitable for table service), place 2 slices of toasted bread.
4) Ladle 2 ounces of warm Hot Brown Sauce over toasted bread.
5) Divide the ham among the 6 baking dishes.
6) Divide the roast turkey among the 6 dishes.
7) Ladle 2 ounces warm Hot Brown Sauce over the turkey.
8) Place 2 slices of bacon on top of each dish.
9) Place a tomato slice in the middle of each dish.
10) Ladle 2 more ounces of Hot Brown Sauce.
11) Bake in oven for 10-12 minutes.
12) Remove and serve.

SERVES 6

Hot Brown Sauce

INGREDIENTS

1 tablespoon butter, melted

1 tablespoon flour

2 cups heavy cream

2 cups chicken broth

2 tablespoons roux

2 cups white cheddar cheese, shredded

METHOD

1) Make a roux by melting the butter in a small sauté pan, stirring in flour and cooking over low heat for about 5 minutes, stirring often. Remove from heat and set aside for later use.
2) Place cream and chicken broth in a small saucepan. Place pan on high heat and bring to a boil, then reduce heat to a simmer.
3) Stir in 2 tablespoons of the roux. Continue to simmer for about 5 minutes.
4) Stir in cheese.
5) Remove from heat. Can be made ahead of time and stored in refrigerator. Reheat when needed.

YIELDS 5 CUPS

Breakfast Home Fries

INGREDIENTS

12-15 medium-sized
new potatoes

1 ½ cups mixed bell
peppers (red, yellow and
green), small-diced

1 cup yellow onion,
small-diced

2 sticks butter

1 tablespoon salt

½ tablespoon freshly-
ground black pepper

METHOD

1) Preheat oven to 350 degrees Fahrenheit.

2) Rinse new potatoes with cool water. Place on a sheet tray and bake for 15 minutes. Remove from oven and let cool.

3) Cut new potatoes into quarters.

4) Place all ingredients into a large skillet over medium heat. Sauté for 10-12 minutes, stirring often.

SERVES 6

Ruby Red Grapefruit Brûlée

The crispy burned sugar crust on my Ruby Red Grapefruit Brûlée puts a fun twist on the traditional breakfast side.

INGREDIENTS

1 whole ruby red grapefruit

6-8 teaspoons sugar

Blackberries or strawberries for garnish

METHOD

1) Place grapefruit on cutting board and slice very small slices off the top and bottom of the grapefruit.

2) Slice the grapefruit in half. Place the grapefruit on a paper towel-lined surface, cut-sides down, for 2-3 minutes. This is done to absorb excess liquids, which allows for better caramelization of the fruit.

3) Move the grapefruit halves to a metal sheet pan. Place about 1 teaspoon of sugar on top of each grapefruit half, then gently melt sugar with a butane torch. When the sugar is caramelized, place another teaspoon of sugar on top of each grapefruit and caramelize a second time. Repeat process a third time.

4) Garnish each with a fresh blackberry or strawberry half. May be made up to 20 minutes before serving.

SERVES 2

Crispy Shiitake "Bacon" Omelet

This simple omelet is stuffed with Brie cheese and sautéed spinach and then topped off with my crispy shiitake "bacon." While there is no actual bacon in the omelet, the cooking process of the shiitakes results in a crunchy, bacon-like flavor to round off this vegetarian brunch item.

INGREDIENTS

Pan release spray, as needed

4 large eggs, cracked

2 ounces milk

⅛ teaspoon white pepper

½ teaspoon salt

¼ cup raw spinach, chopped

2-3 thin slices Brie cheese

METHOD

1) Place cracked eggs, milk, white pepper and salt in a blender and blend for about 30 seconds.

2) Place a 7-8-inch non-stick omelet pan over medium heat. Spray with a little pan release spray and pour egg mixture into the pan.

3) Cook for about 1 minute and scrape sides of the pan with a heat-proof spatula to release egg from the pan. As you scrape the sides down and push the cooked egg to the center of the pan, swirl the pan so that the raw egg mixture comes into contact with the edges of the pan.

4) Repeat this process continually until the egg mixture is evenly cooked.

5) Carefully flip the omelet over and place spinach and Brie on the bottom side of the cooked omelet.

6) Slide the omelet halfway on to the serving plate, then flip the other half of the omelet over itself.

7) Top off omelet with a small handful of crispy shiitakes and serve.

SERVES 1

Crispy Shiitake "Bacon"

Crispy shiitakes make a great substitution for bacon. I often use them to top off salad greens, egg dishes and shiitake-seared beef tenderloin.

INGREDIENTS

1 pound fresh whole shiitake mushroom caps (use largest available)

4 cups vegetable oil

2 tablespoons finely-ground salt (not kosher)

METHOD

1) Place a large heat-proof container (big enough to hold hot oil after cooking mushrooms) to one side for later use. Put a strainer inside the container to catch mushrooms as the oil passes through.

2) Remove stems from shiitakes. Slice mushrooms very thin, focusing on consistency of size.

3) Place the 4 cups of vegetable oil in a large sauté pan.

4) Preheat oil to 250 degrees Fahrenheit.

5) While stirring, add mushrooms a little at a time to the hot oil until all are in the pan.

6) Stir often. Fry mushrooms for about 10-12 minutes. Mushrooms will reduce in size and turn darker.

7) Pour the oil and mushrooms through the strainer into the heat-proof container. Lift strainer and shake off excess oil. Dump mushrooms on top of a paper towel-lined sheet tray.

8) Season with salt.

9) Allow mushrooms to cool at room temperature. May be made up to 2 hours before serving.

YIELDS 1 CUP

Our Daily Bread

Skillet cornbread, yeast rolls and biscuits. These wonderful baked goods are true Southern legends. The recipes are easy to make and will provide the final touches to your own Bluegrass Table.

OUR DAILY BREAD

Southern Cornbread

Calumet Baking Powder Biscuits

Cloverleaf Yeast Rolls

Beaten Biscuits

Southern Cornbread

Cornbread is best when cooked in a hot iron skillet.

INGREDIENTS

2 cups yellow cornmeal

½ cup flour

2 teaspoons baking powder

1 teaspoon baking soda

1 teaspoon salt

1½ cups buttermilk

2 whole eggs

4 tablespoons unsalted butter

METHOD

1) Preheat oven to 425 degrees Fahrenheit.

2) Place 10- or 12-inch iron skillet in oven.

3) In a large bowl, mix all dry ingredients.

4) Mix the buttermilk and eggs in another bowl.

5) Pour the wet mixture over the dry mixture and stir until fully incorporated.

6) Carefully remove skillet from oven and stir in butter to coat the inside of the skillet evenly.

7) Pour cornbread batter into skillet and place in oven. Bake for 20-25 minutes.

8) Remove from oven. Cut into wedges. Serve hot.

SERVES 12

Cooking Notes: Left-over cornbread can be made into Cornbread Croutons (page 31) and used for breading for King Crab Cornbread Cakes (page 175).

Calumet Baking Powder Biscuits

Calumet Baking Powder Company was established in 1889 in Chicago by my great-great-grandfather, William Monroe Wright. The company was named after the Native American Indian word for a peace pipe. In 1929, the business was sold to the General Foods Corporation for an astounding $40 million. From these profits, the Calumet Farm racing dynasty was born – the single most successful racing stable in American history, with eight Kentucky Derby winners. William Wright was also the first cousin of Wilbur and Orville Wright.

INGREDIENTS

2 cups flour

2 teaspoons Calumet Baking Powder

½ teaspoon salt

4 tablespoons chilled butter

⅔ cup milk

METHOD

1) Preheat oven to 450 degrees Fahrenheit.

2) Sift flour, baking powder and salt into a large bowl.

3) Using a fork, cut the chilled butter into the flour mixture.

4) Pour milk into the bowl and stir gently to form dough.

5) Turn dough out onto a lightly-floured surface and knead for about 1 minute.

6) Using a rolling pin, roll out dough to ½-inch thick.

7) Using a 2-inch biscuit cutter, cut out biscuits, dipping the cutter in flour between each cut.

8) Place cut biscuits on sheet tray, then roll out scraps and repeat the cutting process, adding to sheet tray until all dough is used.

9) Bake biscuits for 12-15 minutes. Serve hot from the oven.

YIELDS 1 DOZEN 2-INCH BISCUITS

Cloverleaf Yeast Rolls

INGREDIENTS

1 package dry active yeast

¼ cup warm water

¾ cup hot milk

3 tablespoons shortening

4 tablespoons sugar

1 teaspoon salt

1 egg, beaten

3 ¾ cups flour

2 sticks butter, melted

METHOD

1) Dissolve yeast in the warm water and set aside.

2) In a large bowl, mix hot milk, shortening, sugar and salt. Allow mixture to cool to room temperature.

3) Add dissolved yeast and beaten egg to the milk mixture.

4) Stir in flour a little at a time until dough forms a ball and frees up from the sides of the bowl.

5) Turn dough out onto a lightly-floured surface. Knead the dough by hand for about 15 minutes. Dough is kneaded enough when it has become smooth and elastic. Place dough in a large bowl rubbed with melted butter. Brush top of dough with melted butter. Cover with plastic wrap, and allow the dough to rise at room temperature for approximately 1 hour. Dough should double in size. If not doubled in size, allow more time.

6) Press down on the dough with your hand to flatten the dough slightly and release large air bubbles. Use your hand to form dough balls about 1-inch thick. Brush the insides of a standard size cupcake baking pan. Place 3 small dough balls in each hole, and brush the tops of the dough with melted butter. Allow dough to rise for another 45 minutes to an hour.

7) Place the rolls into a preheated 400 degrees Fahrenheit oven and bake for 15-20 minutes. Brush top of rolls with melted butter while they are still hot. Serve rolls while still warm.

YIELDS 2 DOZEN ROLLS

Beaten Biscuits

This old-time recipe was developed before the invention of baking powder and requires a lot of work. Do not make this recipe if you are not committed to the long, hard work needed to get the dough to the proper consistency. This is by far the most physical recipe in the book, but the end results are worth the work. Pre-made beaten biscuits are available throughout the South and can be substituted.

INGREDIENTS

4 cups flour

1 teaspoon salt

¼ cup shortening

2 tablespoons room temperature butter

1 cup cold milk

METHOD

1) Preheat oven to 400 degrees Fahrenheit.

2) Knead all ingredients by hand in a large bowl until dough is formed. Transfer dough to a sturdy, floured work surface. Beat the dough with a firm blunt instrument such as a wooden hammer handle or thin rolling pin about 25-30 times. Fold dough over itself like a book.

3) Repeat beating another 25-30 times and fold again. The entire beating process should be continued for about 30 minutes. The objective of all of this hard work is to trap very small pockets of air into the dough, providing the dough with a simple form of leavening. As the dough approaches being fully beaten, the texture will acquire a silky quality.

4) When the dough has been fully beaten, use a rolling pin to roll dough out to ¾-inch thick. Cut the dough with a 2-inch biscuit cutter, dusted with flour, between each cut. Place the cut biscuits on a buttered sheet tray. Pierce each biscuit 3 times with a fork.

5) Bake the biscuits for about 20 minutes. Biscuits should be lightly browned on the outside and slightly doughy in the middle. Remove from oven and serve immediately.

YIELDS 2 DOZEN BISCUITS

Signature Sides

Family reunions, neighborhood gatherings and potluck dinners are very common in the South. They often suffer from too many guests bringing the same items, or bringing items prepared in an unimaginative fashion. I will give the reader new options and ideas for stand-out dishes. My signature Southern sides include homemade Salt and Vinegar Potato Chips, Smoked Cheddar Macaroni and Cheese, Wilted Limestone Bibb Lettuce, Crawfish Corn Pudding and Crispy White Cheddar Grits.

SIGNATURE SIDES

Corn Whipped Potatoes

Jasmine Rice

Wilted Limestone Bibb Lettuce

Crawfish Corn Pudding

Soybean Succotash

Crispy White Cheddar Grits

Goat Cheese Scalloped Potatoes

Sugar Snap Peas

Butter-Poached Asparagus

Skillet Cornbread Cakes

Maple-Mustard Slaw

Green Beans

Salt and Vinegar Potato Chips

Bacon-Wilted Baby Spinach

Fresh Horseradish-Creamed Spinach

Horseradish Cream

Smoked Cheddar Macaroni and Cheese

Foie Gras Bread Pudding

Mashed Potatoes

Roasted Garlic Mashed Potatoes

Roasted Garlic Purée

Corn Whipped Potatoes

Puréed roasted corn adds a sweet flavor to these mashed potatoes.

INGREDIENTS

8-10 ears fresh yellow corn in the husk

10 cups sliced peeled potatoes (about 4 pounds)

1 gallon cold water

1 tablespoon salt

¾ cup melted butter

½ cup warm heavy cream

1 teaspoon salt

½ teaspoon ground white pepper

1½ cups roasted yellow corn purée

METHOD

1) Preheat oven to 350 degrees Fahrenheit.
2) Place corn, still in the husk, on a sheet tray and roast in the oven for 10-12 minutes.
3) Remove from the oven and allow it to cool.
4) Shuck the corn from the husks.
5) Cut kernels from the cob.
6) Purée corn in a food processor to a smooth paste.
7) Peel and uniformly slice potatoes.
8) Place in a large pot and cover with cold water and 1 tablespoon salt.
9) Place on stove top on high heat. Bring to a boil and reduce heat to a simmer. Cook for 10-12 minutes or until potatoes are tender.
10) Pour potatoes into a colander in a sink and allow to thoroughly drain for 3-4 minutes.
11) Add butter and heavy cream
12) Mash the cooked potatoes by hand or with a mixer, until smooth.
13) Season with salt and white pepper.
14) Stir in roasted corn purée.

SERVES 6 TO 8

Pairing notes: *Coffee-Seared Pork Chops with Corn Whipped Potatoes and Maker's Mark Red-Eye Gravy*

Cooking notes: *Corn can be roasted and puréed a day ahead.*

Jasmine Rice

I love the nutty taste and smell of jasmine and Basmati rice. When cooking these types of rice, I prefer to use a rice cooker instead of a pot on a stovetop. The ease and convenience of the rice cooker make it a necessity in any well-equipped kitchen.

INGREDIENTS

4 cups jasmine or Basmati rice

5 cups cool water

Spray pan release, as needed

2 bay leaves

2 2-inch stalks of celery

½ yellow onion, peeled with core intact for easy removal

1 tablespoon vegetable oil

2 tablespoons butter

2 teaspoons salt

METHOD

1) Measure rice and place in a fine-mesh strainer. Run cool water over rice until liquid runs clear, washing off excess starch. Allow water to drain thoroughly.

2) Use the pan release to coat the cooking surface of the rice cooker. Place rice, water, bay leaves, celery, onions and vegetable oil in the rice cooker and turn on. When the rice is done, the rice cooker will automatically turn off. Remove bay leaves, celery and onion. Add butter and salt and fluff with a fork.

SERVES 6 TO 8

Wilted Limestone Bibb Lettuce

INGREDIENTS

3-4 heads Bibb lettuce

4 tablespoons Browned Butter, chilled, cut into ¼-inch cubes (page 75)

½ cup Caramelized Onions (page 75)

1 teaspoon kosher salt

½ teaspoon freshly-ground black pepper

METHOD

1) Remove roots from the Bibb lettuce, rinse in cool water and shake off excess liquid. Pick Bibb leaves from core.

2) Preheat large sauté pan over high heat.

3) Add Browned Butter cubes to the hot sauté pan and quickly follow with the Caramelized Onions and Bibb lettuce. Cook for about 3 minutes while continuously tossing.

4) Remove the pan from the heat and serve.

SERVES 6

Crawfish Corn Pudding

Corn pudding, a standard in Kentucky kitchens, utilizes the state's largest cash crop, but all corn puddings are not created equal. Fresh corn is a must. Blend this traditional dish with Creole influences by adding cooked crawfish tails. This recipe also works well with shrimp, lobster, crab or just simply served plain.

INGREDIENTS

6 cups fresh corn,
cut off the cob

2 cups cooked
crawfish tails

1 cup small-diced yellow onion, sautéed in a little butter

2 cups milk

½ cup sugar

2 tablespoons salt

1 teaspoon ground white pepper

¼ cup yellow cornmeal

6 whole eggs

METHOD

1) Preheat oven to 350 degrees Fahrenheit.

2) Butter an oven-proof baking dish.

3) Mix all ingredients. Pour mixture into the baking dish. Cover with aluminum foil.

4) Bake for 20 minutes. Remove foil and continue to bake for another 10-15 minutes until cooked through.

SERVES 6 TO 8

Cooking notes: *This dish can be made about an hour before serving and held in a 200-degree Fahrenheit oven. (In such a situation, you will need to shorten the final cooking time by about 10 minutes).*

Pairing notes: *Skillet-Blackened Salmon, Crawfish, Corn Pudding and Soybean Succotash.*

Soybean Succotash

Succotash is normally a casserole-style dish made with lima beans and corn. In my recipe, I have replaced the lima beans with soybeans because I like the flavor and texture better. The soybeans also retain their bright green color, when cooked.

INGREDIENTS

1 cup frozen shelled soybeans, also called Edamame

1 cup fresh corn, cut from the cob

1 cup diced canned tomatoes, strained

½ cup Caramelized Onions (page 75)

1 tablespoon butter

1 tablespoon salt

½ tablespoon freshly-ground black pepper

METHOD

1) Place all ingredients in a small sauté pan and heat throughout on medium heat.

SERVES 6 TO 8

Crispy White Cheddar Grits

Grits were originally produced by Native American Indians and are commonly eaten throughout the South. Produced from dried corn which has been soaked in water to remove the germ and the hull, this soaked kernel is then dried again and ground into a coarse-ground meal. The dried meal is then boiled with water to produce a polenta-like, corn-based porridge. To widen the appeal of grits, cook them with a good-flavored stock, heavy cream and white cheddar cheese. Then allow the cooked grits to cool and harden. These grits are pan-fried to produce a crispy outer texture while the insides remain creamy.

INGREDIENTS

2 cups grits, not instant

5 cups Shrimp or Chicken Stock (pages 59, 60) or vegetable stock

2 cups heavy cream

2 cups white cheddar cheese

1 tablespoon salt

½ tablespoon ground white pepper

3 cups cornmeal

2 cups vegetable oil

METHOD

1) Place stock/broth and cream in a 2-quart pot. Place over high heat and bring to a boil.

2) Stir in the grits and lower heat to a simmer. Cook for about 20 minutes.

3) Stir in cheese, salt and white pepper. Continue to simmer for another 10 minutes.

4) Taste the grits and notice the texture. When the grits have a smooth, creamy feel in your mouth, they are done. If the grits still have too much texture, add a cup of water and continue to cook them.

5) Pour the cooked grits onto a sheet pan about 1½-inches thick and allow them to cool in the refrigerator.

6) When the grits are thoroughly cool and firm, cut into 3- to 4-inch circles or squares. These cut grits can be made a few days prior to serving and kept in the refrigerator.

7) Dust the cut grits with cornmeal. Set them aside until ready to fry.

8) Preheat the oil to about 350 degrees Fahrenheit in a large sauté pan or preheat a small tabletop deep fat fryer to 350 degrees. In small batches, fry the grits to a golden brown, approximately 2-3 minutes per side.

SERVES 6 TO 8

Goat Cheese Scalloped Potatoes

Scalloped potatoes are a type of casserole, combining thin slices of potatoes, cheese and cream. Southerners often prepare scalloped potatoes for special holiday meals such as Christmas or Thanksgiving. We use locally-produced Capriole goat cheese for this traditional Southern dish, but any good quality goat cheese will do.

INGREDIENTS

3 tablespoons melted butter

5 pounds peeled, thin-sliced potatoes

1 tablespoon salt

1 teaspoon freshly-ground black pepper

3 pounds goat cheese

1 tablespoon freshly-picked thyme

2 cups heavy cream

METHOD

1) Preheat oven to 375 degrees Fahrenheit.

2) Brush a 9 x 9-inch baking dish with the butter.

3) Layer the baking pan with potatoes, cream, thyme, goat cheese, salt and pepper.

4) Cover the dish with plastic wrap and press down with your hands to pack the casserole. Remove plastic wrap and discard.

5) Cover with aluminum foil and bake, covered, for about 25-30 minutes. Remove foil and continue to cook for another 20 minutes or so. Potatoes should be tender, but not over-cooked and mushy.

6) Remove from the oven and let them set, at room temperature, for another 20 minutes.

7) May be served at this time or be reheated for another time.

SERVES 12

Cooking notes: *Place baking dish on a sheet pan to catch any over-run during the cooking process. This simple step will prevent your oven from smoking, leaving a big mess to clean up.*

180

Sugar Snap Peas

Sugar Snap Peas are best when they are just barely cooked. This recipe has two cooking steps, but keeps the peas bright green and crunchy. Cutting the peas and exposing the insides provides the dinner with extra visual excitement.

INGREDIENTS

3 cups fresh
sugar snap peas

6 cups water

1 tablespoon salt

Ice bath (6 cups water
and 6 cups ice)

3 tablespoons butter,
melted

1 teaspoon salt

METHOD

1) Wash off peas in cool water.

2) Prepare an ice water bath

3) Place water and salt in a medium-sized pot with a lid, and bring to a full rolling boil.

4) Remove lid from pot and quickly drop in the snap peas, then give them a stir. Immediately dump the contents into a colander to drain water. Transfer the peas into the prepared ice bath and allow them to cool.

5) Drain the chilled peas from the ice bath.

6) Cut each snap pea on an extreme bias from top to bottom to expose the inner peas. After cutting, place in refrigerator until last-minute cooking. This step can be done a few hours before serving.

7) At time of serving, place the peas and melted butter in a large sauté pan. Gently warm the peas over low heat, being careful not to over-cook. Plate and serve.

SERVES 6

Butter-Poached Asparagus

INGREDIENTS

¾ cup water

4 sticks chilled butter, each stick cut into 8 even slices to create a total of 32 slices

24-30 stalks asparagus, bottoms trimmed

1½ teaspoons salt

¼ teaspoon ground white pepper

METHOD

1) Pour water into a small saucepan. Place pan on high heat and bring to a boil. Remove from heat and whisk in 2 slices of butter until fully melted. Add 2 more slices of butter and continue to whisk gently until melted. Repeat process until half of the total butter has been melted. Return pot to high heat for about 20 seconds and remove. Continue to whisk in the remainder of the butter, a little at a time.

2) Season butter with salt and pepper.

3) Place butter mixture and asparagus in metal baking dish. Cook on low heat for about 12 minutes (cooking time will vary depending on size of asparagus). Wiggle the dish back and forth every few minutes to ensure even heating. The butter should reach and not exceed 190 degrees Fahrenheit and should never come to a boil. Reduce heat, if needed.

4) Remove asparagus when tender and light green in color. Serve while hot.

SERVES 6

Skillet Cornbread Cakes

INGREDIENTS

1 cup Weisenberger
Mill cornmeal

½ cup flour

1 teaspoon baking powder

1 cup buttermilk

2 eggs

1 cup fresh corn,
cut from the cob

1 tablespoon small-diced
red bell peppers

1 tablespoon thinly-sliced
scallions

1 teaspoon salt

½ teaspoon freshly-ground
black pepper

4 tablespoons vegetable oil

METHOD

1) Preheat oven to 300 degrees Fahrenheit.

2) Mix the cornmeal, flour, baking powder and salt in a medium-sized bowl.

3) Add eggs, corn, bell peppers, scallions, salt and black pepper. Mix well.

4) Preheat a large skillet with the vegetable oil. Ladle the batter into six cakes.

5) Sauté each cake for about 3 minutes. Keep warm in oven until serving.

YIELDS 6 3-INCH CAKES - SERVES 6

Maple-Mustard Slaw

INGREDIENTS

6 cups thinly-sliced
green cabbage

½ cup grated,
peeled carrots

½ cup thinly-sliced
red onion

¼ cup thinly-sliced
red bell pepper

½ cup thinly-sliced
yellow bell pepper

½ tablespoon kosher salt

½ cup Maple-Mustard
Dressing (page 31)

¼ cup Maple-Mustard
Glaze (page 30)

1 tablespoon brown sugar

½ cup mayonnaise

METHOD

1) Mix green cabbage, carrots, red onions, bell peppers and salt in a large mixing bowl. Let sit for 1 hour and then squeeze out excess moisture with your hands, placing squeezed mixture into a medium-sized mixing bowl.

2) Mix with remaining ingredients.

3) Store in a refrigerator until serving for up to 3 days. Slaw is best when at least a day old.

YIELDS 6 CUPS

Green Beans

INGREDIENTS

1 pound French green beans or haricots verts, a small thin variety of green bean

½ gallon water

2 tablespoons salt

2 tablespoons butter

METHOD

1) Bring water and salt to a boil in a medium-sized pot on high heat.

2) Submerge green beans into boiling water. Let beans cook in boiling water for about 4-5 minutes. Dump beans and boiling water into a colander in a sink.

3) Place the beans in a large bowl and toss with the butter. Serve while still hot.

SERVES 6 TO 8

Salt and Vinegar Potato Chips

These potato chips require a 24-hour soaking process and special equipment, but are worth the time and effort. If the salt and vinegar flavor is not for you, just skip the final seasoning and experiment with other seasonings

INGREDIENTS

6-8 large Idaho potatoes

½ gallon cider vinegar

½ gallon water

Vegetable oil, to fill tabletop fryer, as needed

¼ cup iodized salt

4 tablespoons Tamanoi Sushinoko sushi seasoning mix

Ingredients notes:
Tamanoi Sushinoko is available at most Japanese markets. It is a small yellow package filled with a powder used to season sushi rice, which works great to season my chips.

METHOD

1) Wash potatoes in cool water. Peel, if desired. I prefer skin on.

2) Using a deli-style slicer or mandolin, slice potatoes into long slices, each about 1/8-inch thick.

3) Place sliced potatoes in a large pot. Place pot in a sink with running hot water. Mix up the chips and water together with your hands to rinse off the natural potato starch thoroughly. Continue for 2-3 minutes.

4) Pour rinsed potatoes into a colander and drain off water.

5) Rinse out large pot. Add the ½ gallon of vinegar and ½ gallon of water. Add rinsed potatoes and give a quick stir. Refrigerate for 24 hours.

6) Preheat small tabletop fryer to 300 degrees Fahrenheit.

7) Pour soaked potatoes into a colander to remove liquid. Allow to drain thoroughly. Pat down chips with a paper towel to help remove moisture, which you do not want to add to the fryer.

8) In small batches, add the dried potatoes into the fryer, stirring and flipping chips often. Fry the chips for about 4-5 minutes or until a light golden tan is achieved. Remove chips from fryer and lay out on a paper towel-lined sheet tray. Season the chips with the spice mixture, immediately after removing from fryer.

9) Store chips in an airtight container for up to 3 days.

SERVES 6 TO 8

Bacon-Wilted Baby Spinach

INGREDIENTS

10 slices raw bacon

6 cups baby spinach, about ¾ pound

2-3 tablespoons rendered bacon fat

2 teaspoons cider vinegar

1 teaspoon salt

½ teaspoon freshly-ground black pepper

METHOD

1) Preheat oven to 400 degrees Fahrenheit.

2) Lay bacon out on sheet tray and bake for about 5 minutes, or until bacon is about halfway cooked. Remove tray and let cool. Cut each piece of bacon in half and stack in piles of 6. Slice the half pieces of bacon into thin ribbons, ¼-inch wide.

3) Transfer 2-3 tablespoons of rendered bacon fat from tray into a large skillet or sauté pan. Add bacon ribbons and cook over medium heat, stirring often until bacon is crispy. Remove and set aside.

4) Pour out excess bacon fat and return to heat. Add spinach, cider vinegar, salt and pepper.

5) Cook just to wilt spinach, about 2-3 minutes. Serve immediately.

SERVES 6

Fresh Horseradish-Creamed Spinach

INGREDIENTS

2¾ pounds spinach
(1 gallon packed)

2 cups Horseradish Cream
(recipe below)

1 cup Swiss cheese, grated

2 teaspoons salt

1 teaspoon freshly-
ground black pepper

METHOD

1) Preheat oven to 400 degrees Fahrenheit.

2) In a large pot, add about 1 cup of water and place on high heat. Add spinach while constantly stirring and flipping spinach around with a pair of tongs. Cook spinach just long enough to wilt the spinach. Dump the wilted spinach into a large colander and run cold water over spinach to cool.

3) Squeeze spinach with hands to remove excess water. This step should be repeated 3 times to remove the moisture.

4) Place the squeezed spinach on a cutting board and roughly chop.

5) Mix all ingredients together. Place in an oven-proof dish and bake for 10-12 minutes.

YIELDS 10 SERVINGS

Horseradish Cream

INGREDIENTS

½ pound peeled, puréed
fresh horseradish root
(about 2 cups)

1 quart heavy cream

METHOD

1) Mix horseradish and cream together in a small saucepot. Place over medium heat. Allow cream to simmer for about 20 minutes. Remove from heat and allow it to cool to room temperature.

2) Strain the cream mixture through a fine-mesh strainer. Reserve the cream for later use and discard the horseradish.

YIELDS ABOUT 3 CUPS

Smoked Cheddar Macaroni and Cheese

INGREDIENTS

6 cups cooked macaroni or other bite-size pasta

4 cups heavy cream

1 tablespoon cornstarch

1 tablespoon cool water

2 egg yolks

1¼ pounds finely-shredded, smoked cheddar cheese

1 tablespoon salt

1 teaspoon freshly-ground black pepper

1 cup breadcrumbs

2 tablespoons chopped parsley

2 tablespoons melted butter

METHOD

1) Preheat oven to 400 degrees Fahrenheit.
2) Cook pasta in salted boiling water until just a little underdone.
3) Place cream in medium pot and bring to a boil over high heat.
4) Mix cornstarch and cool water in a small bowl. Pour into pot while stirring. Reduce heat and simmer for 3-4 minutes.
5) Whisk in 1 pound of shredded cheese. Stir until melted.
6) Ladle out about ½ cup of cream into a small bowl. Whisk egg yolks, 1 at a time, into the bowl. Pour contents back into the pot and simmer for about 2-3 minutes. Remove from heat.
7) Place cooked pasta into baking dish. Pour cream sauce over and stir.
8) Mix breadcrumbs, parsley and butter together.
9) Scatter breadcrumb mixture over pasta and sauce.
10) Scatter the remaining ¼ pound of cheese over the top.
11) Bake for 20 minutes.

SERVES 6 TO 8

Foie Gras Bread Pudding

INGREDIENTS

2 tablespoons olive oil

2 cups diced onions

2 cups diced celery

2 cups diced carrots

1 tablespoon
chopped garlic

1 tablespoon
chopped fresh thyme

1 cup dry white wine

2 cups half-and-half

12 ounces small-diced
foie gras

10 whole eggs

4 cups half-and-half

1 gallon ½-inch cubed
brioche bread, dried out in
a low-temperature oven

½ cup chopped, fresh flat
leaf parsley

2 tablespoons salt

2 teaspoons freshly-
ground black pepper

METHOD

1) Preheat oven to 375 degrees Fahrenheit.

2) In a large sauté pan, sauté the onions, celery, carrots and garlic in olive oil until tender. Add fresh thyme and white wine. Simmer for 3-4 minutes to cook off alcohol. Remove from heat and allow mixture to cool.

3) Place cooled vegetables in a blender with 2 cups half-and-half. Pulse blender on and off a few times to produce a coarse blend. Remove from blender and set aside.

4) Place foie gras, eggs and 4 cups half-and-half in blender. Pulse blender on and off a few times to produce a coarse blend. Remove from blender and set aside.

5) In a large mixing bowl, mix all ingredients together. Allow bread to soak up liquids for about 20 minutes.

6) Place the mixture into a buttered baking dish. Cover pan with aluminum foil. Bake covered for 20 minutes. Remove foil and continue to bake another 15-20 minutes.

SERVES 12

Mashed Potatoes

Everyone loves freshly-made mashed potatoes. If you use heavy cream instead of milk, the potatoes wil have an added richness. If you are watching your fat intake, use 2% or skim milk.

INGREDIENTS

10 cups sliced, peeled potatoes (about 4 pounds)

1 gallon cold water

1 tablespoon salt

¾ cup melted butter

½ cup warm heavy cream

1 teaspoon salt

½ teaspoon ground white pepper

METHOD

1) Peel and uniformly slice potatoes.

2) Place in a large pot and cover with cold water and 1 tablespoon salt.

3) Place on stove top on high heat. Bring to a boil and reduce heat to a simmer. Cook for 10-12 minutes or until potatoes are tender.

4) Pour potatoes into a colander in a sink and allow to drain thoroughly for 3-4 minutes.

5) Pour potatoes into a bowl and add butter and cream.

6) Mash the cooked potatoes by hand or with a mixer, until smooth.

7) Season with salt and white pepper.

SERVES 6 TO 8

Roasted Garlic Mashed Potatoes

INGREDIENTS

1 Mashed Potatoes
(page 192)

6 tablespoons Roasted
Garlic Purée (recipe below)

METHOD

1) Prepare Mashed Potatoes recipe.

2) Stir in Roasted Garlic Purée (recipe below) and serve.

SERVES 6 TO 8

Roasted Garlic Purée

INGREDIENTS

30-40 peeled garlic cloves

About 2 cups olive oil

METHOD

1) Place the garlic cloves in a small saucepan or sauté pan. Cover garlic with olive oil.

2) Place over medium heat and bring the oil to a boil. Turn off the heat and let stand until cool to the touch. Garlic cloves should be soft to the touch. If not, cook a few minutes more.

3) Strain garlic cloves and purée in food processor.

4) Refrigerate until needed. Can be made up to three days ahead of time.

SERVES 6 TO 8

Dramatic Endings

Southerners always have a taste – and room – for something sweet. There are so many wonderful regional desserts that have long histories and are suggestive of place. Some take advantage of summer's bounty — cobblers topped with drop biscuits, for instance. Others share fall's bounty in winter — an Appalachian dried apple stack cake is a good example. Sweeteners are used interchangeably, whether sorghum, honey, molasses, brown sugar or white sugar. The choice is based upon no choice. But something sweet is always made to share and is most likely to disappear right after these words are uttered, "Oh, I couldn't eat another bite!"

My Flaming Butterscotch-Bourbon Crème Brûlée has the usual vanilla bean added to its custard, but it is the addition of Butterscotch Schnapps that lifts the flavor to a new height. A teaspoon of Booker's high-proof, single-barrel Kentucky Bourbon whisky, flamed over a caramelized sugar crust, sends it soaring.

Bread pudding with a Bourbon sauce is an old standard of the Bluegrass kitchen. In mine, I use not bread, but a heavenly creation from a bakery that specializes in old-fashioned fried doughnuts. Their stale doughnuts are simply soaked in a mixture of eggs, cream and vanilla, then baked. My Spalding's Bakery Doughnut Bread Pudding is finished off with Wild Turkey American Honey Liqueur. Sadly, now that the secret is out, I will have to go even earlier to stand in line before they sell out.

My Cherry Molasses Stack Cake is a new adaptation of the traditional Appalachian apple stack cake. The cooled, rich, chewy molasses cake is sliced into thin layers horizontally. Then I reassemble the cake, spreading my Old Fashioned Cherry Relish between each layer. Slice the stack vertically to display the cake's array of colors.

Yams do double duty in a Southern kitchen. They make a delicious side dish or an equally delicious dessert. In my re-imagined cheesecake, roasted yams are mixed with cream cheese, sugar and eggs and baked in a graham cracker crust. The Candied Yam Cheesecake is finished with toasted marshmallows, maple syrup and toasted pecans.

Chocolate Bourbon Brownie is one of the signature flavors of my ultra premium ice cream line. I have been experimenting with this for 10 years. Some ideas work. Some really, really don't. I've shared the basics and my best flavor profiles. Experiment with adding flavor to the base. Even your worst attempt is still ice cream!

DRAMATIC ENDINGS

Flaming Butterscotch-Bourbon Crème Brûlée

Cherry Molasses Stack Cake

Cherry Filling for Cherry Molasses Stack Cake

Chocolate Pot Pies

Chocolate Pot Pie Lids

Candied Yam Cheesecake

Spalding's Doughnut Bread Pudding

Wild Turkey American Honey Liqueur Sauce

Caramel Pound Cake with Caramel Sauce

Jonathan's Vanilla Bean Ice Cream

Chocolate Bourbon Brownie Ice Cream

Chocolate Ganache Cake with Pecan Brittle Crust

Flaming Butterscotch-Bourbon Crème Brûlée

This recipe replaces the ordinary crusted custard with the extraordinary, and it lends an unexpected excitement to dessert. We first use Butterscotch Schnapps to flavor the standard custard. Then I develop a caramelized sugar crust with a butane torch. Finally, pour just a touch of Booker's Bourbon on top, then flame the confection tableside for a truly dramatic presentation.

INGREDIENTS

3 egg yolks

3 whole eggs

½ cup sugar

2 cups heavy cream

2 tablespoons sour cream

4 tablespoons
Butterscotch Schnapps

½ tablespoon
vanilla extract

Sugar, as needed

1 tablespoon Booker's
Single-Barrel Bourbon

METHOD

1) Preheat oven to 300 degrees Fahrenheit.

2) In a mixing bowl, add the yolks, whole eggs and sugar. Whip to a light fluffy consistency.

3) Place heavy cream and sour cream in a medium-sized pot and heat over medium heat to a very light boil. Remove from heat.

4) Take 3-4 ounces of the warm cream mixture and stir gradually into the egg and sugar mixture. When thoroughly incorporated, repeat this step 3 times. Add remainder and mix well.

5) Pour the mixture through a fine-mesh strainer.

6) Portion the mixture into 6 3-4-ounce oven-proof dishes.

7) Place the dishes into a small roasting pan.

8) Fill roasting pan with hot water up to the halfway mark on the batter-filled, oven-proof dishes.

9) Cover roasting pan with aluminum foil. Poke a finger-sized hole in each corner to allow steam to escape.

10) Place pan in the oven and bake for about 10-12 minutes. Check for doneness. Cook longer, if custard has not set.

11) Remove from oven and allow the crème brûlée to cool to room temperature. Remove from water bath and place in the refrigerator. (This step can de done as far as 2 days in advance)

12) At time of serving, sprinkle 1 tablespoon sugar over the top of the custard. Using a butane torch, slowly wave the torch over the top of the custard and caramelize the sugar topping. Repeat to develop a sugar crust.

13) Pour 1 tablespoon Booker's Single-Barrel Bourbon over sugar crust.

14) Flame the Bourbon tableside. Let fire fully extinguish before eating.

YIELDS 6 4-OUNCE PORTIONS

Cherry Molasses Stack Cake

The apple stack cake originated in the Appalachian Mountains of Eastern Kentucky. This many-layered cake was usually made with dried apples and sorghum. In the mountains, the cake was often referred to as wedding cake. Family and friends would donate dough to the bride's family. The dough was then rolled into thin layers and baked. The number of layers in the cake represented the popularity of the bride. My pastry chef, David Schmidt, created his own version of this Kentucky classic, using dried cherries and molasses.

INGREDIENTS

3 cups all-purpose flour

1¼ teaspoons baking soda

1 teaspoon ground cinnamon

½ teaspoon ground cloves

¼ teaspoon ginger powder

1½ cups vegetable oil

2 cups sugar

3 eggs

⅓ cup molasses

1 teaspoon salt

1 teaspoon vanilla extract

Cherry Filling (page 201)

METHOD

1) Preheat oven to 350 degrees Fahrenheit.

2) Spray a 9 x 9 jellyroll pan with pan release and line with parchment paper.

3) Sift all dry ingredients except sugar. Set aside.

4) Beat sugar and oil together with a whisk in a large bowl.

5) Add 1 egg at a time to the bowl. Scrape down sides of bowl between each addition.

6) Stir in molasses and vanilla.

7) Stir in sifted dry ingredients.

8) Spread batter into prepared pan and bake for 25 minutes. Remove and cool to room temperature.

9) Turn cake out of pan by inverting onto a cutting board. Lift pan off cutting board. Peel parchment paper from cake.

10) Trim the outer edges of the cake and discard.

11) Cut cake crosswise into 4 equal rectangles.

12) Place 1 layer of the cake on the cutting board. Spread ⅓ of cherry filling evenly over cake. Place another layer of cake on top of the first and repeat the process until you have 4 layers of cake and 3 layers of cherry filling.

13) Wrap entire cake with plastic wrap and refrigerate for at least 8 hours, for up to 3 days.

14) At time of serving, unwrap and slice cake into ½-inch slices.

SERVES 12

Cherry Filling for Cherry Molasses Stack Cake

INGREDIENTS

1 pound dried cherries

3 cups apple juice

1 cinnamon stick

5 whole cloves

3 x 3 inch square of cheesecloth

METHOD

1) Place cinnamon and cloves in cheesecloth. Tie a knot in the cheesecloth to secure contents. This is done so you can easily remove spices before you purée.

2) Place the cherries, apple juice and cheesecloth sachet into a medium saucepan. Bring mixture to a boil on high heat on the stovetop. Reduce heat and simmer for 5-6 minutes, stirring occasionally until most of the liquid is absorbed.

3) Remove from heat and allow to cool at room temperature. Remove cheesecloth sachet.

4) Place mixture in a food processor and purée.

5) Store cherry purée in an airtight container in the refrigerator until needed. Can be made up to 2-3 days in advance.

YIELDS ABOUT 6 CUPS

Chocolate Pot Pies

INGREDIENTS

18 ounces semi-sweet chocolate

10 ounces butter

2 tablespoons Bourbon

6 egg yolks

4 whole eggs

¼ cup sugar

Chocolate Pot Pie Lids (recipe below)

Vanilla Bean Ice Cream (page 211)

Chocolate sauce, as needed

METHOD

1) Preheat oven to 400 degrees Fahrenheit.

2) Brush the inside of 8 4-ounce ramekins with butter. Set aside.

3) Melt the chocolate in a double boiler, with the butter and Bourbon.

4) Mix the egg yolks, whole eggs and sugar for 2-3 minutes in a mixer bowl with a paddle attachment. Pour the melted chocolate mixture into the mixer bowl. Mix just well enough to blend.

5) Fill each ramekin almost to the top.

6) Place a Chocolate Pot Pie Lid on each.

7) Bake pot pies for 10-12 minutes (The outer centimeter of the batter should be cooked and set, while the middle of the pot pie should be runny.)

8) Top each off with a scoop of my Vanilla Bean Ice Cream and drizzle with chocolate sauce.

SERVES 8 (ONE 4-OUNCE RAMEKIN PER PERSON)

Chocolate Pot Pie Lids

INGREDIENTS

¼ teaspoon baking powder

1¼ cups flour

¼ teaspoon salt

¼ cup cocoa powder

1 stick butter

½ cup sugar

1 egg

¼ teaspoon vanilla extract

METHOD

1) Sift all dry ingredients. Set aside.

2) Cream the sugar and butter together for 2-3 minutes in a mixer bowl with a paddle attachment. Stop the mixer, add the egg and vanilla, and mix until thoroughly incorporated. Stop the mixer, scrape down the sides of the bowl and restart.

3) Slowly add the dry ingredients to the mixer bowl. Allow the dough to form.

4) Remove the mixture from the mixer bowl, cover with plastic wrap and refrigerate for at least 1 hour.

5) Dust work surface with a little cocoa powder and roll dough out to about ⅛-inch thick. Cut the dough with a round cookie cutter that is approximately the same size as the individual baking dishes. Gather scraps left over from cutting, then re-roll and cut more lids.

6) Place cut Pot Pie Lids on sheet tray and refrigerate until needed. Can be made up to 3 days ahead of time.

Candied Yam Cheesecake

INGREDIENTS

3 cups graham cracker crumbs

½ pound melted butter

1½ pounds cream cheese, softened at room temperature

¾ cup brown sugar

¾ pound roasted sweet potato purée

1 teaspoon vanilla extract

½ teaspoon ground allspice

½ teaspoon ground cinnamon

1 teaspoon salt

5 whole eggs

½ cup heavy cream

Yellow and red food color, as needed

2 cups marshmallow fluff

1 cup maple syrup

1 cup chopped pecans

METHOD

1) Preheat oven to 375 degrees Fahrenheit.

2) Roast 4-5 large sweet potatoes in the oven for about 30 minutes or until tender inside. Remove from oven and allow potatoes to cool at room temperature. When sweet potatoes are cool to the touch, remove skin and purée in a food processor to produce a smooth consistency. Weigh out the needed ¾-pound of purée needed for recipe.

3) Mix graham cracker crumbs and melted butter together. Spray a 9-inch spring form pan and spray well with non-stick aerosol spray. Cover bottom of pan with graham cracker crumbs and press down with hands to pack crust tight. Place pan in the oven and cook crust for about 5 minutes. Remove from oven and let cool to room temperature.

4) When the pan is cool to the touch, cover outside of the spring form pan with 2 sheets of aluminum foil, all the way up the sides of the pan. Fold foil above the rim back over the outside of the pan. This step is taken to ensure no water will leak into the pan and make the crust soggy during the cooking process.

5) Place softened cream cheese and brown sugar into a mixer bowl and cream mixture with a paddle attachment. Be sure to stop the mixer and thoroughly scrape down the sides of the bowl. Restart to ensure the cream cheese becomes thoroughly mixed and has no lumps.

6) Stop the mixer and add the roasted sweet potatoes, spices, salt and vanilla extract, then cream the mixture once again. Repeat the scrape-down process.

7) Next, while the machine is running on low speed, add 1 egg at a time. After all the eggs have been added, stop the mixer and repeat the scrape-down process once again.

8) Next, while machine is mixing on low speed, slowly add the cream.

9) Stop mixer and remove about 1 cup of the mixture, pouring it into a small bowl. Mix in a few drops of red and yellow food coloring

204

and mix with a spoon. Blend the colored mixture back into the remaining batter. Repeat this process to achieve a light orange color similar to the color of the roasted sweet potatoes. Work slowly and carefully with the food color, using only a few drops at a time, so as not to over-color the batter.

10) Pour finished batter into the spring form pan. Place the pan in a high-walled baking dish that is at least 1 inch taller than the spring form pan. Fill the baking dish with warm water, halfway up the side of the spring form pan. Cover the top of the baking dish with a sheet of aluminum foil. Poke 4 finger-size holes in the foil to allow steam to escape. The foil will protect the top of the cheesecake from browning or burning and will help with the cooking process. If the holes are not provided, the cheesecake will be steamed and will overcook very easily.

11) Preheat oven to 300 degrees Fahrenheit.

12) Carefully place the foil-wrapped pan into the oven and bake for 45 minutes. Check doneness every 10 minutes thereafter. Use a toothpick to poke the middle of the cake to check if the cake is done. Toothpick will come out clean, with nothing sticking to it, if the cake is done. If the cake is not done, return it to the oven, covered.

13) When the cake is done, remove the foil cover and let it cool at room temperature while still in the water bath. After cake becomes cool to the touch, remove from the water bath and place it in the refrigerator. The cheesecake should be refrigerated for at least 24 hours to fully set.

14) To remove the cake from the pan, set the cake out at room temperature for about an hour. Unhook the ring and slowly lift it from the cake. Next take 2 spatulas and pry them between the crust and the bottom pan and lift the cake up and place it on a cutting board. Slice the cake into 12 slices with a long slicing knife dipped into hot water. Wipe with a paper towel in between each slice.

15) Place a tablespoon of marshmallow fluff on each slice and toast with a butane torch to achieve a slightly toasted or burned appearance. Top cake slices off with some toasted pecans and a little maple syrup drizzle.

YIELDS 1 9-INCH CAKE

Spalding's Doughnut Bread Pudding

The Spalding family has been producing its old-fashioned doughnuts in Lexington for three generations. Started in 1928 by B.J. and Zelma Spalding, with a recipe developed from experimentation in their backyard, Spalding's has become legendary within the Bluegrass and is a must on visitors' to-do lists. Come early. They sell out daily.

INGREDIENTS

1 gallon dried, glazed doughnuts, cut into ½-inch cubes, (about 18-20 doughnuts)

10 eggs

1 quart half-and-half

2 cups brown sugar

2 teaspoons vanilla extract

1 teaspoon salt

2 tablespoons melted butter

METHOD

1) Preheat oven to 350 degrees Fahrenheit.

2) Crack eggs into a large mixing bowl. Add half-and-half, brown sugar, vanilla extract and salt. Mix well.

3) Add dried doughnut cubes. Allow the doughnuts to soak in the custard base for 45 minutes.

4) Brush the insides of a 6 x 9-inch baking dish with the butter.

5) Pour mixture into the baking dish, cover with aluminum foil and bake in the oven for 30 minutes. Remove foil and bake another 15 minutes.

6) Ladle Wild Turkey American Honey Liqueur Sauce before serving.

SERVES 12

Preparation notes: *I suggest cutting bread pudding into 2 x 2-inch squares. The doughnut-shaped version shown in the photo opposite results in a large amount of scraps.*

Wild Turkey Honey Liqueur Sauce

INGREDIENTS

½ pound melted butter

4 tablespoons water

2 cups sugar

½ cup Wild Turkey American Honey Liqueur

½ teaspoon freshly-ground nutmeg

¼ teaspoon salt

2 eggs

METHOD

1) Add melted butter, water, sugar, Wild Turkey, nutmeg, and salt in a small saucepan. Place pot over low heat and stir until sugar has melted into the sauce.

2) Remove from heat and whisk vigorously until sauce becomes light and fluffy.

3) Add the eggs to the sauce and return it to medium heat. Simmer sauce, whisking often, until sauce thickens. Remove from heat and keep at room temperature until serving.

YIELDS 3 ⅓ CUPS - SERVES 12

Caramel Pound Cake

INGREDIENTS

¾ pound softened, room- temperature butter

3 cups sugar

2 cups flour, for dusting baking pans

9 eggs at room temperature

4 cups flour

2 teaspoons baking powder

1 teaspoon salt

2 cups Caramel Sauce (page 210)

METHOD

1) Follow provided Caramel Sauce recipe.

2) Soften 3 sticks (¾ pound) of butter and bring 9 eggs to room temperature.

3) Preheat oven to 325 degrees Fahrenheit.

4) Melt 1 stick (¼ pound) of butter in a microwave oven for about 30 seconds. Brush the insides of 2 6-cake mini bundt cake pans with melted butter. Place the buttered molds into the refrigerator for about 5 minutes. Remove from the refrigerator, reapply a second coating of butter to the molds and refrigerate them for another 5 minutes. Remove them from the refrigerator and sprinkle the 2 cups of flour into one of the molds. Shake to cover the insides of the mold. Flip the mold over and turn the excess flour into the second mold and shake it to cover the buttered surface of the second tray. Discard excess flour. Place both molds back into the refrigerator for another 5 minutes.

5) Sift the 4 cups of flour, salt and baking powder. Set aside for later use.

6) Place the softened butter and sugar into a mixer bowl fitted with a paddle attachment. Cream mixture on high speed for about 3-4 minutes, until light and fluffy.

7) Set mixer to lowest speed and crack 1 egg at a time into the creamed mixture. Stop the mixer, scrape down the sides of the bowl and return to low speed. Mix for another 2 minutes until fully incorporated.

8) Slowly add the sifted flour mixture into the mixing bowl. Mix on low speed for about 2 minutes. Stop the mixer and scrape down the sides, then return to mixing at low speed for another 2 minutes.

9) While mixer is still running slowly, add 2 cups of the Caramel Sauce. Stop the mixer and scrape down the sides. Turn it on again, just long enough to thoroughly incorporate the sauce.

10) Portion the cake batter into the mold, filling only about ¾ of the way to the top.

11) Place filled cake molds into the oven and bake for about 12 minutes. Rotate pans about halfway through the cooking process to ensure even cooking. Test cake for doneness, using a toothpick. Poke the middle of the cake, looking for the toothpick to come out clean, indicating cakes are done. Cook for another few minutes and test again.

12) Remove from the oven and allow the pans to cool for about 5 minutes. Quickly flip pans over onto a surface covered with parchment paper. Carefully remove pans from the cakes. Allow the cakes to cool to room temperature.

YIELDS 12 5-OUNCE MINI BUNDT CAKES

Caramel Sauce

INGREDIENTS

1 tablespoon
light corn syrup

4 cups sugar

1 cup water

2 ounces butter

2 cups heavy cream

METHOD

1) Place corn syrup, sugar and water in a small pot and place on medium heat. Allow mixture to simmer until the mixture develops a dark tan color, about 10-12 minutes.

2) Whisk in butter until fully melted and incorporated.

3) Remove from heat. Allow mixture to cool for a few minutes and then slowly whisk in the heavy cream. Use caution while stirring in the cream, as mixture will release steam in the stirring process.

4) Allow caramel to cool to room temperature before adding to cake batter.

5) If making ahead of time, store caramel in refrigerator for up to week. Reheat gently in a double boiler until sauce comes to a liquid state.

YIELDS 4 CUPS

Jonathan's Vanilla Bean Ice Cream

INGREDIENTS

1 vanilla bean

1⅓ quarts
half-and-half

1 quart heavy
whipping cream

¾ pound egg yolks
(about 18 large
egg yolks)

1¼ pounds sugar

1 teaspoon salt

1 tablespoon
vanilla extract

METHOD

1) Cut vanilla bean in half lengthwise. Scrape the insides to remove the seeds. Set aside, reserving the seeds.

2) In a large, thick-bottomed pot, place the half-and-half, heavy cream, vanilla bean and the scraped-out seeds. Place the pot on the stove on medium heat.

3) Place the yolks and sugar into a large bowl. Using a hand mixer, whip the mixture until it reaches a light fluffy consistency, about 4-5 minutes.

4) When the cream mixture is just a little shy of a boil, remove from heat. Ladle out about a cup of the cream and mix it into the yolks. Stir until thoroughly combined. Repeat 3 times. Pour yolk mixture back into the cream and stir until thoroughly combined.

5) Return the mixture to the stove on medium heat. Stir mixture every few minutes. Using a thermometer, continue to cook until mixture reaches 180 degrees Fahrenheit. Remove from heat.

6) Strain mixture through a fine-mesh colander.

7) Place ice cream base in refrigerator and allow to cool thoroughly.

8) Stir in the vanilla and salt.

9) The ice cream base is now ready to freeze. (Follow ice cream machine instructions)

10) Store in freezer for 24 hours to allow ice cream to set properly.

YIELDS 1½ GALLONS

Chocolate Bourbon Brownie Ice Cream

INGREDIENTS

5 ⅓ cups half-and-half

1 quart heavy cream

¾ pound egg yolks
(about 2 dozen
eggs needed)

1¼ pounds sugar

1 cup cocoa powder

4 ounces semi-sweet
chocolate

1 teaspoon salt

1 tablespoon
vanilla extract

8 cups diced,
dried brownie cubes

1 cup Bourbon

METHOD

1) Using your favorite brownie recipe or a store-bought mix, follow instructions and produce brownies. Allow brownies to cool, cut into ½-inch cubes. Place cut brownies on sheet tray and bake at 200 degrees Fahrenheit for about 15 minutes to dry out. Remove from oven and set aside.

2) Place egg yolks, sugar and cocoa powder in mixing bowl and whip with a whisk attachment for about 5 minutes, until a light-colored fluffy texture is achieved. Set aside, until needed.

3) In a large, thick-bottomed pot, mix the half-and-half and heavy cream. Place the pot over medium heat, stirring often. Heat mixture to 180 degrees Fahrenheit and then stir in the whipped egg yolks and semi-sweet chocolate, stirring constantly. Bring mixture back up to 180 degrees, remove from heat and pass through a fine-mesh colander. Chill mixture in an ice bath to cool.

4) Place dried brownies out on a sheet pan. Pour the 1 cup Bourbon evenly over the brownies, set aside.

5) Follow ice cream machine instructions to freeze. Do not attempt to freeze ice cream until thoroughly chilled. When ice cream is frozen, scoop into storage container layered with Bourbon-soaked brownies. Store in freezer for 24 hours to properly set.

YIELDS ABOUT 2 GALLONS

Chocolate Ganache Cake

INGREDIENTS

Pecan Brittle Crust
(page 216)

3 cups chopped
pecan brittle

3 cups graham
cracker crumbs

1 teaspoon salt

1¼ cup melted butter

½ pound dark chocolate

4 cups heavy cream

2 tablespoons Bourbon

METHOD

1) Make Pecan Brittle Crust.

2) Chop chocolate and place in a medium-sized stainless steel bowl. Place bowl over a small pot of simmering water. Allow chocolate to melt thoroughly, about 10 minutes. Remove from heat.

3) Place 2 cups of heavy cream in a mixer bowl with a whip attachment and whip to soft peaks. Set aside.

4) Place the other 2 cups heavy cream in a small microwavable container and microwave cream for about 30 seconds to heat it. Pour the heated cream and Bourbon into the melted chocolate and stir to incorporate.

5) Fold whipped cream into chocolate mixture. Be sure to mix thoroughly until smooth.

6) Pour chocolate into the crust-lined spring form pan. Refrigerate for about 6 hours or until chocolate has set up firm.

7) To remove from the pan, unhook the spring form pan buckle and carefully lift the ring from the cake. Using 2 spatulas, lift the cake from the bottom of the pan and place it on a cutting board. Slice the cake into 12 slices with a long slicing knife, dipping it into warm water and wiping it with paper towels between each slice. Keep refrigerated until serving.

YIELDS 1 9-INCH CAKE

Pecan Brittle Crust

INGREDIENTS

½ cup water

1 cup light corn syrup

2 cups sugar

½ pound butter

2 teaspoons salt

1½ teaspoons
baking soda

3 cups
chopped pecans

5 cups graham
cracker crumbs

1 pound butter, melted

METHOD

1) Place water, corn syrup and sugar in a small saucepan. Place the pot over medium heat. Stir occasionally until sugar is melted and fully incorporated.

2) Whisk in the butter until mixture is blended.

3) Continue to simmer until mixture has reached 305 degrees Fahrenheit on a candy thermometer.

4) Stir in pecans, salt and baking soda. Mix well.

5) Pour mixture on a sheet tray and allow it to cool.

6) When thoroughly cooled and hardened, break into small, dime-sized pieces.

7) Place in food processor and purée into a coarsely-ground meal.

8) Toss results of step #7 and remaining ingredients together in a large bowl.

9) Press crust down in the bottom of a 9-inch spring-form pan.

10) Place in refrigerator for ½ hour.

YIELDS 2 9-INCH CRUSTS

Cooking notes: This recipe makes enough crust for 2 9-inch cakes. Store extras in refrigerator for up to 2 weeks. After refrigeration, set crust out at room temperature to soften before packing into spring form pan.

Un-Commonwealth Cocktails

Kentucky was designated a Commonwealth by the Kentucky Constitution of 1792. My "Un-Commonwealth" cocktails all focus on the utilization of Kentucky's native spirits, which can blend with other popular cocktails or give a new twist to produce some uncommon results.

Some of my signature cocktails are as follows. The Bourbon Alexander is an after-dinner cocktail made with my ultra premium Vanilla Bean Ice Cream and Godiva Liqueur. The Belle Brezing Martini, named after the famous Lexington madam who ran a brothel in the same building in which my restaurant is now located, is a delicious mix of orange, pomegranate and cranberry. The Peachy Bourbon Sour is a whiskey sour-inspired cocktail made with fresh peaches. Jonathan's fresh cherry Old Fashioned was a finalist in the 2008 Kentucky Bourbon Festival Drink Challenge. The Kentucky Speedball combines Ale-8-1, a locally-made, highly caffeinated soft drink with premium Bourbon. And, finally, the Bluegrass Mint Julep – while not so uncommon – is a Kentucky tradition.

In 1999, eight historic Bourbon distilleries came together to create the Bourbon Trail – the Kentucky equivalent of California's wine region tours and Scotland's whiskey trails. It has been a boon for tourism and a much-deserved tribute to a true Kentucky original.

UN-COMMONWEALTH COCKTAILS

Belle Brezing Martini

Bourbon Alexander

Peachy Bourbon Sour
Peach Sweet-and-Sour Mix

Jonathan's Old Fashioned

Kentucky Speedball

Bluegrass Mint Julep

Belle Brezing Martini

Nationally known as a madam, Belle Brezing was born June 16, 1860, and passed away August 11, 1940. She ran a number of brothels in the downtown Lexington area. The character of Belle Watling from Gone with the Wind was said to be loosely based on Brezing. She operated her bordello for a short time at 194 North Upper Street, which is the same building in which Jonathan at Gratz Park is now located. This martini was developed in her honor, with the help of my good friend and colleague T. J. Cox.

INGREDIENTS

2 ounces Bourbon

1 ounce Grand Marnier

1 ounce
pomegranate liqueur

Splash of cranberry juice

Twist of orange

METHOD

1) Pour first four ingredients over ice and shake vigorously.

2) Strain into a chilled martini glass.

3) Use the orange side of the twist to coat the rim of the glass. Go around the rim at least ten times. The essence of orange brings bright flavors to the cocktail.

SERVES 1

Bourbon Alexander

The traditional Brandy Alexander was the inspiration for my Bourbon Alexander. It was developed with the help of my friend Gail Bennett, the marketing director from WUKY public radio, for the fundraiser "Bourbon, Boys and Toys." The main component of the cocktail is my ultra premium Vanilla Bean Ice Cream. Godiva Chocolate Liqueur is exchanged for dark crème de cacao and Bourbon exchanged for the brandy. This cocktail is best served after a meal as a dessert replacement.

INGREDIENTS

2 ounces
Maker's Mark Bourbon

2 ounces Godiva Liqueur

5 ounces Jonathan's
Vanilla Bean Ice Cream
(about 2 ½ scoops)
(page 211)

¹⁄₁₆ teaspoon fresh
grated nutmeg

METHOD

1) Place Bourbon, Godiva Liqueur and ice cream in blender.

2) Purée until smooth.

3) Pour into 8-ounce brandy snifter.

4) Dust top with freshly-grated nutmeg.

SERVES 1

Peachy Bourbon Sour

INGREDIENTS

2½ ounces Bourbon

1 ounce Peach Schnapps

2½ ounces Peach Sweet-and-Sour Mix (recipe below)

Lemon wedge

Peach slices

METHOD

1) Pour Bourbon, Peach Schnapps, and Peach Sweet-and-Sour Mix over ice in a highball or pint glass.
2) Stir to incorporate.
3) Garnish with a lemon wedge and peach slices.

SERVES 1

Peach Sweet-and-Sour Mix

INGREDIENTS

6 lemons, juiced

6 limes, juiced

5 tablespoons Peach Preserves (page 23)

METHOD

1) Mix all ingredients, store in refrigerator until needed.

YIELDS ABOUT 2 CUPS, ENOUGH FOR 6 COCKTAILS

Jonathan's Old Fashioned

In response to the 2008 Bourbon Festival Drink Challenge, it was important to improve on the maraschino cherries customarily used for an Old Fashioned. The use of fresh macerated cherries brings new life to an old favorite. Even though the cocktail did not win best of show, we had a lot of fun testing the recipe.

INGREDIENTS

2 tablespoons juice from Old Fashioned Macerated Fresh Cherries (page 137)

2 Old Fashioned Macerated Cherries (page 137)

1 slice navel orange, cut into half-moons

3 ounces Makers' Mark Kentucky Straight Bourbon Whisky

3-4 dashes Angostura bitters

A splash of ginger ale

METHOD

1) In a large cocktail glass, muddle together: 2 macerated cherries, 1 half-moon slice of navel orange, the juice from the macerated cherries and 2 dashes of Angostura bitters.

2) Fill the glass with ice and pour in the whisky. Stir to incorporate the ingredients.

3) Top with ginger ale.

SERVES 1

Kentucky Speedball

Ale 8-1 is a family-owned, Winchester, Kentucky-made soda, which has been in production since 1926. It has a fruity ginger ale-like flavor, with more caffeine and less carbonation than most sodas. The Ale 8-1 bottling company ships out over 1.5 million cases a year, most of which is consumed within Kentucky, Ohio and Indiana. Kentuckians are fond of mixing the local product with another one of its local beverages, Bourbon.

INGREDIENTS

2 ounces Bourbon

4 ounces Ale 8-1

Crushed ice to fill glass

Lemon and lime to garnish

METHOD

1) Fill 12-ounce highball glass with crushed ice.
2) Pour 2 ounces Bourbon over ice.
3) Fill glass with 4 ounces Ale 8-1.
4) Stir gently, garnish with lemon and lime wheels.

SERVES 1

Bluegrass Mint Julep

While the mint julep is not so "uncommon," it is Kentucky's most famous drink, perfect for spring and summertime entertaining.

INGREDIENTS

6-8 fresh mint leaves

1 ounce simple syrup

3 ounces Bourbon

A splash of club soda

Mint to garnish

METHOD

1) Place mint leaves and simple syrup in a julep cup and muddle together.
2) Fill cup with crushed ice.
3) Pour Bourbon over ice.
4) Stir.
5) Splash with club soda.
6) Garnish with mint.

SERVES 1

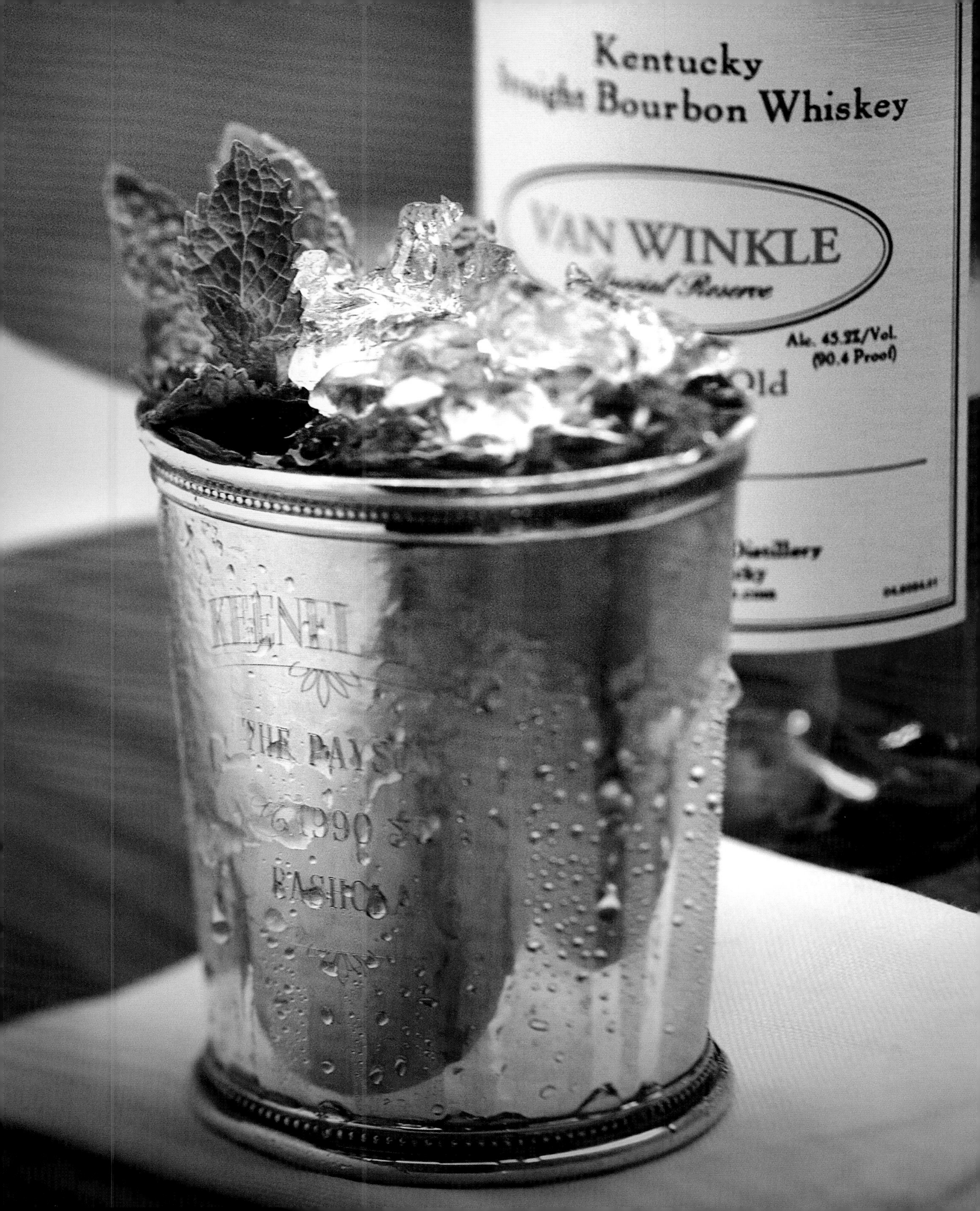
Kentucky
Bourbon Whiskey
VAN WINKLE
(90.4 Proof)

INDEX

Aioli, Roasted Corn, 79
Arugula Oil, 54
    in Chilled Potato Vichyssoise with Capriole Goat Cheese
      and Arugula Oil, 53
Asparagus, Butter-Poached, 182
Asparagus-Chive Deviled Eggs (in Deviled Egg Trio), 71
Asparagus, Pickled Pepper-Marinated, 33
"Bacon," Crispy Shiitake, 157
"Bacon" Omelet, Crispy Shiitake, 156
Bacon-Wilted Baby Spinach, 188
    in Sorghum-Glazed Seared Sea Scallops, 122
Banana Pepper Mayonnaise, Fire-Roasted, 69
Bananas Foster Sauce, 145
    in Cornmeal Waffles with Bananas Foster Sauce
      and Toasted Pecans, 144
Barbeque Sauce, Maple-Mustard, 110
Barbeque Sauce, Simple Tomato, 111
Barbequed Yellow Fin Tuna, 108
Batter, Kentucky Ale, 40
Beans, Green, 185
Beaten Biscuits, 168
    in Seared Foie Gras, 91
Beef Carpaccio, Pepper-Seared, 95
Beef, Shiitake-Dusted Tenderloin Medallions, 131
Belle Brezing Martini, 222
Biscuits
    Beaten, 168
    Calumet Baking Powder, 164
Bison and Black-Eyed Pea Chili, Kentucky, 52
Bison Brisket, Kentucky Bourbon Barrel Ale-Braised, 128
Bisque, Roasted Tomato, with Buttermilk Whipped Cream
    and Brioche Croutons, 55
Blackberry Balsamic Preserves, 91
    in Seared Foie Gras, 91
Black-Eyed Pea Chili, Kentucky, Kentucky Bison and, 52
Black-Eyed Pea-Crusted Trout, 104
Black-Eyed Peas, Crispy, 27
Bluegrass Mint Julep, 232
Bourbon Alexander, 224
Bourbon Barrel Ale Beer Cheese, Kentucky, 85
Bourbon Barrel Ale-Braised Bison Brisket, Kentucky, 128
Bourbon Sour, Peachy, 227
Bourbon Soy Dipping Sauce, 82
Bread Pudding, Spalding's Doughnut, 206
Breakfast Home Fries, 152
Brioche Croutons, 56
    in Roasted Tomato Bisque with Buttermilk Whipped Cream
      and Brioche Croutons, 55

Brittle, Cayenne Pecan, 22
Brittle Salad, Cayenne Pecan, 21
Brown Beef Stock, 61
    in Jonathan's Kentucky Burgoo, 58
    in Horseradish Gravy, 126
    in Caramel-Peppercorn Sauce, 133
Browned Butter, 75
    in Mushrooms and Dumplings, 73
    in Wilted Limestone Bibb Lettuce, 176
Burgoo, Jonathan's Kentucky, 58
Butter, Browned, 75
Buttermilk Dressing, 18
    in Fried Green Tomato Salad, 14
Buttermilk Whipped Cream, 56
Buttermilk Whipped Cream,
    in Roasted Tomato Bisque, with Brioche Croutons, 55
    in Sorghum-Glazed Seared Sea Scallops, 122
Butter-Poached Asparagus, 182
Butterscotch-Bourbon Crème Brûlée, Flaming, 198
Caesar Salad Dressing, 26
    in Grilled Caesar Salad, 25
Cakes
    Caramel Pound, with Caramel Sauce, 209
    Cherry Molasses Stack, 200
Calumet Baking Powder Biscuits, 164
Candied Yam Cheesecake, 204
Caramel Pound Cake with Caramel Sauce, 209
Caramel Sauce, 210
    in Caramel Pound Cake with Caramel Sauce, 209
Caramelized Onions, 75
    in Mushrooms and Dumplings, 73
    in Kentucky Bourbon Barrel Ale Beer Cheese, 85
    in Wilted Limestone Bibb Lettuce, 176
    in Soybean Succotash, 178
Caramel-Peppercorn Base, 133
Caramel-Peppercorn Sauce, 133
    in Shiitake-Dusted Beef Tenderloin Medallions, 131
Cayenne Pecan Brittle, 22
    in Cayenne Pecan Brittle Salad, 21
Cayenne Pecan Brittle Salad, 21
Cheddar, Macaroni and Cheese, Smoked, 190
Cheese
    Capriole Goat and Arugula Oil,
     in Chilled Potato Vichyssoise, 53
    Crispy White Cheddar Grits, 179
    Goat, Scalloped Potatoes, 180
    Jonathan's Pimento, 87
    Kentucky Bourbon Barrel Ale Beer, 85

Pimento, Grit Fries, 66
	Smoked Cheddar Macaroni and, 190
Cheesecake, Candied Yam, 204
Cherry Filling for Cherry Molasses Stack Cake, 201
	in Cherry Molasses Stack Cake, 200
Cherry Molasses Stack Cake, 200
Cherry Relish
	Duck Confit with Old Fashioned, 135
	Old Fashioned, 136
Cherries, Old Fashioned Macerated, 137
	in Old Fashioned Cherry Relish, 136
Chicken, Rock Salt-Roasted, 114
Chicken Salad, 35
	in Chicken Salad-Stuffed Tomato with
	Pickled Pepper-Marinated Asparagus, 33
Chicken Salad-Stuffed Tomato with
	Pickled Pepper-Marinated Asparagus, 33
Chicken Stock, 59
	in Chilled Potato Vichyssoise with Capriole Goat Cheese
	and Arugula Oil, 53
	in Sheltowee Farm Shiitake Egg Drop Soup, 57
	in Mushrooms and Dumplings, 73
	in Country Ham Carbonara, 113
	in Shrimp and Grits, 121
	in Crispy White Cheddar Grits, 179
Chili, Kentucky Bison and Black-Eyed Pea, 52
Chilled Potato Vichyssoise with Capriole Goat Cheese
	and Arugula Oil, 53
Chips, Salt and Vinegar Potato, 187
Chocolate Bourbon Brownie Ice Cream, 212
Chocolate Ganache Cake with Pecan Brittle Crust, 215
Chocolate Pot Pie Lids, 203
	in Chocolate Pot Pies, 203
Chocolate Pot Pies, 203
Chowder, Sweet Corn,
	with Cornmeal-Fried Freshwater Shrimp, 50
Cloverleaf Yeast Rolls, 167
Coffee-Seared Pork Chops, 101
Corn Chowder with
	Cornmeal-Fried Freshwater Shrimp, Sweet, 50
Corn Dog Wedge Salad, Shrimp, 37
Corn Dogs, Shrimp, 38
	in Shrimp Corn Dog Wedge Salad, 37
Corn Pudding, Crawfish, 177
Corn Whipped Potatoes, 174
Cornbread Cakes, King Crab, 77
Cornbread Cakes, Skillet, 183
Cornbread Croutons, 31
	in Hot Smoked Salmon Chop Salad, 29
Cornmeal-Fried Freshwater Shrimp, 51
Cornmeal Waffles with Bananas Foster Sauce
	and Toasted Pecans, 144
Country Ham
	Carbonara, 113
	in Deviled Egg Trio, 70
	Pot Stickers, 80

Crab, King, Cornbread Cakes, 77
Cracker-Fried Oysters, 127
	in Cracker-Fried Oyster-Stuffed Filet, 125
Cracker-Fried Oyster-Stuffed Filet, 125
Cracklings, Pork Jowl, 45
	in Kentucky Hot Slaw, 43
	in Hot Slaw Dressing, 44
Crawfish Corn Pudding, 177
Cream, Buttermilk Whipped, 56
	in Roasted Tomato Bisque, with Brioche Croutons, 55
Crème Brûlée, Flaming Butterscotch-Bourbon, 198
Crispy Black-Eyed Peas, 27
	in Grilled Caesar Salad, 25
	in Black-Eyed Pea-Crusted Trout, 104
Crispy Shiitake "Bacon," 157
	in Shiitake-Dusted Beef Tenderloin Medallions, 131
	in Crispy Shiitake "Bacon" Omelet, 156
Crispy Shiitake "Bacon" Omelet, 156
Crispy White Cheddar Grits, 179
Croutons
	Brioche, 56
	Cornbread, 31
Deviled Egg Trio, 70
	Asparagus-Chive, 71
	Country Ham, 70
	Smoked Salmon, 70
Deviled Thousand Island Dressing, 41
	in Shrimp Corn Dog Wedge Salad, 37
Doughnut Bread Pudding, Spalding's, 206
Duck Confit with Old Fashioned Cherry Relish, 135
Dumplings, Mushrooms and, 73
Dumplings, Potato-Parmesan, 74
	in Mushrooms and Dumplings, 73
Eggs
	Benedict, Southern, 143
	Crispy Shiitake "Bacon" Omelet, 156
	Deviled, Trio, 70
		Asparagus-Chive, 71
		Country Ham, 70
		Smoked Salmon, 70
Traditional Deviled, 73
Fire-Roasted Banana Pepper Mayonnaise, 69
	in Pimento Cheese Grit Fries, 66
Fire-Roasted Banana Pepper Purée, 69
	in Fire-Roasted Banana Pepper Mayonnaise, 69
Flaming Butterscotch-Bourbon Crème Brûlée, 198
Foie Gras, Seared, 91
Foie Gras Bread Pudding, 191
Fresh Horseradish-Creamed Spinach, 189
	in Cracker-Fried Oyster-Stuffed Filet, 125
Fresh Salmon Croquettes, 146
Fried Green Tomato Salad, 14
Fried Green Tomatoes, 17
	in Fried Green Tomato Salad, 14
	in Southern Eggs Benedict, 143

Fries
    Breakfast Home, 152
    Pimento Cheese Grit, 66
Garlic Mashed Potatoes, Roasted, 193
Garlic Purée, Roasted, 193
    in Roasted Garlic Mashed Potatoes, 193
Goat Cheese Scalloped Potatoes, 180
Grapefruit Brûlée, Ruby Red, 154
Gravy, Horseradish, 126
Gravy, Maker's Mark Red-Eye, 102
Green Beans, 185
Green Tomato Piccalilli Relish, 68
    in Pimento Cheese Grit Fries, 66
Grilled Caesar Salad, 25
Grilled Lamb Rack with Mint Julep Jelly, 117
Grits, Crispy White Cheddar, 179
Grits, Shrimp and 121
Ham
    Country (in Deviled Egg Trio), 70
    Country, Carbonara, 113
    Country, Pot Stickers, 80
Hollandaise Sauce, 149
    in Southern Eggs Benedict, 143
Horseradish Cream, 189
    in Fresh Horseradish-Creamed Spinach, 189
Horseradish Gravy, 126
    in Cracker-Fried Oyster-Stuffed Filet, 125
Hot Brown, 150
Hot Brown Sauce, 150
    in Hot Brown, 150
Hot Slaw Dressing, 44
    in Kentucky Hot Slaw, 43
Hot Smoked Salmon Chop Salad, 29
Ice Cream, Chocolate Bourbon Brownie, 212
Ice Cream, Jonathan's Vanilla Bean, 211
Jasmine Rice, 175
Jonathan's Kentucky Burgoo, 58
Jonathan's Old Fashioned, 228
Jonathan's Pimento Cheese, 87
    in Redneck Rockefellers, 87
Jonathan's Vanilla Bean Ice Cream, 211
    in Chocolate Pot Pies, 203
    in Bourbon Alexander, 224
Julep, Bluegrass Mint, 232
Julep Jelly, Grilled Lamb Rack with Mint, 117
Kentucky Ale Batter, 40
    in Shrimp Corndog Wedge Salad, 37
Kentucky Bison and Black-Eyed Pea Chili, 52
Kentucky Bourbon Barrel Ale Beer Cheese, 85
Kentucky Bourbon Barrel Ale-Braised Bison Brisket, 128
Kentucky Hot Slaw, 43
Kentucky Speedball, 230-
King Crab Cornbread Cakes, 77
Lamb Rack with Mint Julep Jelly, Grilled, 117
Lettuce, Wilted Limestone Bibb, 176
Macaroni and Cheese, Smoked Cheddar, 190

Maker's Mark Red-Eye Gravy, 102
    in Coffee-Seared Pork Chops, 101
Maple-Mustard Barbeque Sauce, 110
    in Barbequed Yellow Fin Tuna, 108
Maple-Mustard Dressing, 31
    in Hot Smoked Salmon Chop Salad, 29
Maple-Mustard Glaze, 30
    in Maple-Mustard Slaw, 184
    in Maple-Mustard Hot Smoked Salmon, 30
Maple-Mustard Hot Smoked Salmon, 30
Maple-Mustard Slaw, 184
    in Barbequed Yellow Fin Tuna, 108
Martini, Belle Brezing, 222
Mashed Potatoes, 192
    in Cracker-Fried Oyster-Stuffed Filet, 125
    in Roasted Garlic Mashed Potatoes, 193
Mayonnaise, Fire-Roasted Banana Pepper, 69
Meats
    Beef
        Brown Beef Stock, 61
        Cracker-Fried Oyster-Stuffed Filet, 125
        Pepper-Seared Beef Carpaccio, 95
        Shiitake-Dusted Beef Tenderloin Medallions, 131
    Bison
        Kentucky Bison and Black-Eyed Pea Chili, 52
        Kentucky Bourbon Barrel Ale-Braised Bison Brisket, 128
    Lamb
        Grilled Lamb Rack with Mint Julep Jelly, 117
    Pork
        Coffee-Seared Pork Chops, 101
        Country Ham Carbonara, 113
        Country Ham Pot Stickers, 80
        Country Ham (in Deviled Egg Trio), 70
        Hot Brown, 150
Medallions, Shiitake-Dusted Beef Tenderloin, 131
Mint Julep Jelly, 118
    in Grilled Lamb Rack with Mint Julep Jelly, 117
Mushrooms and Dumplings, 73
Oil, Roasted Garlic, 95
    in Pepper-Seared Beef Carpaccio, 95
Old Fashioned, Jonathan's, 228
Old Fashioned Cherry Relish, 136
    in Duck Confit with Old Fashioned Cherry Relish, 135
Old Fashioned Macerated Cherries, 137
    in Old Fashioned Cherry Relish, 136
    in Jonathan's Old Fashioned, 228
Omelet, Crispy Shiitake "Bacon," 156
Onions, Caramelized, 75
Oysters, Cracker-Fried, 127
Oyster-Stuffed Filet, Cracker-Fried, 125
Peach Preserve Vinaigrette, 23
    in Cayenne Pecan Brittle Salad, 21
Peach Preserves, 23
    in Peach Preserve Vinaigrette, 23
    in Peach Sweet-and-Sour Sauce, 82
Peach Sweet-and-Sour Mix, 227
    in Peachy Bourbon Sour, 227

Peach Sweet-and-Sour Sauce, 82
Peachy Bourbon Sour, 227
Peas
    Crispy Black-Eyed, 27
    Sugar Snap, 181
Pepper-Seared Beef Carpaccio, 95
Pickled Pepper-Marinated Asparagus, 33
Pickled Pepper Vinaigrette, 34
    in Chicken Salad-Stuffed Tomato with
        Pickled Pepper-Marinated Asparagus, 33
Pimento Cheese Grit Fries, 66
Pork Chops, Coffee-Seared, 101
Pork Jowl Cracklings, 45
    in Kentucky Hot Slaw, 43
    in Hot Slaw Dressing, 44
Pot Pies, Chocolate, 203
Pot Stickers, Country Ham, 80
Potato Chips, Salt and Vinegar, 187
Potato-Parmesan Dumplings, 74
    in Mushrooms and Dumplings, 73
Potato-Spun Shrimp, 93
Potatoes
    Goat Cheese Scalloped, 180
    Mashed, 192
    Roasted Garlic Mashed, 193
Poultry
    Chicken
        Chicken Salad, 35
        Chicken Stock, 59
        Chicken Salad-Stuffed Tomato with
        Pickled Pepper-Marinated Asparagus, 33
        Rock Salt-Roasted Chicken, 114
    Duck
        Duck Confit with Old Fashioned Cherry Relish, 135
        Foie Gras
        Foie Gras Bread Pudding, 191
        Seared Foie Gras, 91
    Turkey
        Hot Brown, 150
Preserves
    Blackberry Balsamic, 91
    Peach, 23
Purée, Fire-Roasted Banana Pepper, 69
Redneck Rockefellers, 87
Relish
    Green Tomato Piccalilli, 68
    Tomato Dill, 148
Rice, Jasmine, 175
Roasted Corn Aioli, 79
Roasted Garlic Mashed Potatoes, 193
Roasted Garlic Oil, 95
    in Pepper-Seared Beef Carpaccio, 95
Roasted Garlic Purée, 193
    in Roasted Garlic Mashed Potatoes, 193
Roasted Tomato Bisque with Buttermilk Whipped Cream
    and Brioche Croutons, 55

Rock Salt-Roasted Chicken, 114
Rockefellers, Redneck, 87
Ruby Red Grapefruit Brûlée, 154
Salad Dressings
    Buttermilk, 18
    Caesar Salad, 26
    Deviled Thousand Island, 41
    Hot Slaw Dressing, 44
    Maple-Mustard, 31
    Peach Preserve Vinaigrette, 23
    Pickled Pepper Vinaigrette, 34
Salmon Chop Salad, Hot Smoked, 29
Salmon Croquettes, Fresh, 146
Salmon, Skillet-Blackened, 107
Salmon, Smoked, (in Deviled Egg Trio), 70
Salt and Vinegar Potato Chips, 187
Sauces
    Bananas Foster, 145
    Bourbon Soy Dipping, 82
    Caramel, 210
    Caramel-Peppercorn, 133
    Hollandaise, 149
    Hot Brown, 150
    Maple-Mustard Barbeque, 110
    Peach Sweet-and-Sour, 82
    Sea Scallop Hot Brown, 89
    Simple Tomato Barbeque, 111
    Wild Turkey American Honey Liqueur, 206
Scallop Hot Brown Sauce, Sea, 89
    in Sea Scallop Hot Browns, 88
Scallop Hot Browns, Sea, 88
Scallops, Sorghum-Glazed Seared Sea, 122
Sea Scallop Hot Brown Sauce, 89
    in Sea Scallop Hot Browns, 88
Sea Scallop Hot Browns, 88
Seafood
    Crab
        King Crab Cornbread Cakes, 77
    Crawfish
        Crawfish Corn Pudding, 177
    Oysters
        Cracker-Fried Oysters, 127
        Redneck Rockefellers, 87
    Salmon
        Fresh Salmon Croquettes, 146
        Maple-Mustard Hot Smoked Salmon, 30
        Skillet-Blackened Salmon, 107
        Smoked Salmon (in Deviled Egg Trio), 70
    Sea Scallops
        Sea Scallop Hot Browns, 88
        Sorghum-Glazed Seared Sea Scallops, 122
    Shrimp
        Cornmeal-Fried Freshwater Shrimp, 51
        Potato-Spun Shrimp, 93
        Shrimp and Grits, 121
        Shrimp Corn Dog Wedge Salad, 37

Shrimp Corn Dogs, 38
Shrimp Stock, 60
Trout
    Black-Eyed Pea-Crusted Trout, 104
Tuna
    Barbequed Yellow Fin Tuna, 108
Seared Foie Gras, 91
Sheltowee Farm Shiitake Egg Drop Soup, 57
Shiitake Dust, 132
    in Shiitake-Dusted Beef Tenderloin Medallions, 131
Shiitake-Dusted Beef Tenderloin Medallions, 131
Shiitake Egg Drop Soup, Sheltowee Farm, 57
Shiitake Omelet, "Bacon" in Crispy, 156
Shrimp and Grits, 121
Shrimp Corn Dog Wedge Salad, 37
Shrimp Corn Dogs, 38
    in Shrimp Corn Dog Wedge Salad, 37
Shrimp, Cornmeal-Fried Freshwater, 50
Shrimp, Potato-Spun, 93
Shrimp Stock, 60
    in Sweet Corn Chowder with Cornmeal-Fried
      Freshwater Shrimp, 50
    in Sea Scallop Hot Brown Sauce, 89
Simple Tomato Barbeque Sauce, 111
    in Maple-Mustard Barbeque Sauce, 110
Skillet-Blackened Salmon, 107
Skillet Cornbread Cakes, 183
Slaw
    Kentucky Hot, 43
    Maple-Mustard, 184
Smoked Cheddar Macaroni and Cheese, 190
Smoked Salmon (in Deviled Egg Trio), 70
Sorghum-Glazed Seared Sea Scallops, 122
Soups
    Chilled Potato Vichyssoise, with Capriole Goat Cheese
      and Arugula Oil, 53
    Jonathan's Kentucky Burgoo, 58
    Kentucky Bison and Black-Eyed Pea Chili, 52
    Roasted Tomato Bisque with Buttermilk Whipped Cream
      and Brioche Croutons, 55
    Sheltowee Farm Shiitake Egg Drop, 57
    Sweet Corn Chowder with Cornmeal-Fried
      Freshwater Shrimp, 50
Southern Cornbread, 163
    in Cornbread Croutons, 31
Southern Eggs Benedict, 143
Soybean Succotash, 178
Spalding's Doughnut Bread Pudding, 206
Speedball, Kentucky, 230-
Spinach
    Bacon-Wilted Baby, 188
    Fresh Horseradish-Creamed, 189
Stock
    Brown Beef, 61
    Chicken, 59
    Shrimp, 60

Succotash, Soybean, 178
Sugar Snap Peas, 181
Sweet Corn Chowder with Cornmeal-Fried Freshwater Shrimp, 50
Tomato Barbeque Sauce, Simple, 111
    in Maple-Mustard Barbeque Sauce, 110
Tomato, Chicken Salad-Stuffed, with
    Pickled Pepper-Marinated Asparagus, 33
Tomato Dill Relish, 148
Tomato, Fried Green, Salad, 14
Tomato Piccalilli Relish, Green, 68
Tomatoes, Fried Green, 17
    in Fried Green Tomato Salad, 14
    in Southern Eggs Benedict, 143
Traditional Deviled Eggs, 72
    in Deviled Egg Trio, 70
Trout, Black-Eyed Pea-Crusted, 104
Tuna, Barbequed Yellow Fin, 108
Vanilla Bean Ice Cream, Jonathan's, 211
Vegetables
    Bacon-Wilted Baby Spinach, 188
    Butter-Poached Asparagus, 182
    Crawfish Corn Pudding, 177
    Fresh Horseradish-Creamed Spinach, 189
    Fried Green Tomatoes, 17
    Green Beans, 185
    Maple-Mustard Slaw, 184
    Potatoes
      Breakfast Home Fries, 152
      Corn Whipped Potatoes, 174
      Goat Cheese Scalloped Potatoes, 180
      Mashed Potatoes, 192
      Potato-Parmesan Dumplings, 74
      Roasted Garlic Mashed Potatoes, 193
      Salt and Vinegar Potato Chips, 187
      Soybean Succotash, 178
    Sugar Snap Peas, 181
    Wilted Limestone Bibb Lettuce, 176
Vichyssoise, Chilled Potato, with Capriole Goat Cheese
    and Arugula Oil, 53
Vinaigrette
    Peach Preserve, 23
    Pickled Pepper, 34
      in Chicken Salad-Stuffed Tomato with
        Pickled Pepper-Marinated Asparagus, 33
Waffles, Cornmeal, with Bananas Foster Sauce
    and Toasted Pecans, 144
Wild Turkey American Honey Liqueur Sauce, 206
    in Spalding's Doughnut Bread Pudding, 206
Wilted Limestone Bibb Lettuce, 176
Yellow Fin Tuna, Barbequed, 108